AMERICA'S BEST
HARLEY-DAVIDSON
CUSTOMS

Timothy Remus

Motorbooks International
Publishers & Wholesalers

First published in 1993 by Motorbooks International
Publishers & Wholesalers, PO Box 2, 729 Prospect Avenue,
Osceola, WI 54020 USA

Motorbooks International books are also available at
discounts in bulk quantity for industrial or sales-
promotional use. For details write to Special Sales Manager
at the Publisher's address

Library of Congress Cataloging-in-Publication Data
Remus, Timothy
   America's best Harley-Davidson customs / Timothy
Remus.
     p.   cm.
   Includes index.
   ISBN 0-87938-702-5
   1. Harley-Davidson motorcycle.   2. Harley-Davidson
motorcycle—Customizing.   I. Title.
TL448.H3R44   1993
629.227'5—dc20   92-29760

Printed and bound in Hong Kong

On the front cover: The personal ride of custom builder
Donnie Smith is a bike that was in the works for seven years.

On the back cover: HogZZilla is parked on a remote
bridge; a Donnie Smith creation awaits a run down the drag
strip; and a Dave Perewitz bike is ready to roll after taking
on fuel.

On the frontispiece: The Revolution engine created by
Dave Perewitz using two front cylinders.

On the title page: A Donnie Smith-built Fat Boy custom.

Contents

Acknowledgments

Somehow all the slides I shot last year in South Dakota, all the ideas I've had rattling around in my head, and all the facts about all the motorcycles have once again arranged themselves into a book. Each time this happens it amazes me more than the last. It's time to remember what Mom told me and be sure to say thank you.

Thanks to Donnie and Arlen and Don and Bob and Pete and Al and Dave—all the guys who build the bikes. I know I lied when I said the photo session was only going to take "about an hour," and I know it took a lot longer to get to that great spot for the pictures than I said it would. But you can see now that it was all worth it.

Thanks to Jack in Texas for help in shooting the HogZZilla bikes and to Roy for helping me push them up the hill. And thanks to the lady who owns the De Soda cafe in Spearfish, South Dakota, for letting me hang around all those evenings. (If you stop by be sure to order the chicken, it's great.)

Thanks to Grant and Baby Jane for logistical support during the week of Sturgis. And thanks again to my lovely and talented wife Mary for putting up with my weird hours.

Introduction

This book is a little different than most motorcycle or car books. The difference starts with the way it is organized. But before explaining the organization of the book, I have to back up a little.

After many years of hanging around the men and women who build custom motorcycles and automobiles, I've reached the conclusion that the people who build the machines are at least as interesting as the machines themselves. Further, the personalities of the builders are usually expressed, at least in some small way, in the machines themselves.

So, after writing the Arlen Ness book and meeting many of the builders who are Arlen's peers and often his friends, I got to thinking: What about a book full of custom Harleys, organized not around the bikes but around the men who built the bikes?

Thus, you hold a book with six chapters, each chapter representing a motorcycle builder (or team) and three of his motorcycles. Working within the theme of building the book around the person as well as the machines, each chapter presents a short biography of the builder(s), who he is, how he got hooked on Harleys, and how his bikes are different from the rest.

Each of the builders in the book is a professional builder. Each has considerable experience building custom Harleys. Each runs a shop dedicated to the sales and service of custom Harleys. Most of the shops sell a full range of parts and accessories as well as full bikes.

Some of the builders, men like Arlen and Cory Ness, are well known, while others are more obscure. Two of the men in the book, Bob Bauder and Pete Chapouris, are better known in street rod circles.

What each has in common is the ability and the motivation to build truly wonderful motorcycles. One man might be a better painter and another might be a better machinist, yet each of these men is able to create designs that can only be called revolutionary. These men have one more thing in common: the guts to do it and stick with it long enough to actually learn not only how to build motorcycles but how to make a living building motorcycles.

People have asked how I picked the six men (or teams) covered here. Aside from using the criteria already mentioned, I asked other builders. I queried Donnie Smith and Don Hotop and Arlen Ness, and many more. I asked them who they thought were the best or most significant bike builders in the country. Each of the men in this book was recommended by other builders—each has the respect of his peers.

There were other practical considerations as well. Things like the cost of airfare and the need to get everything done in a reasonable period of time. Because of these "real world" considerations, at least two professional builders of some repute are not included here. But each book has only so many pages, and when you put the Bible on the head of a pin, it gets darned hard to see all the tiny little pictures.

The bikes in the book run the gamut from mild FXRs to wild custom-framed, one-off bikes that rely on Harley-Davidson for the engine and transmission, and that's about all. There are Softails and Hardtails, Shovelheads and Sportsters, and a lot of work that most of us would be very proud to call our own. But again, there was a problem with the real world.

While we have the audacity to call this America's Best, these bikes actually represent the best from each builder that were available for photography.

So, read and enjoy. Appreciate the bikes, but also the wealth of skill and creativity that made them possible.

Chapter 1

Donnie Smith

Worth the Wait: Seven years doesn't seem so long now

Some projects take longer than others. The bike seen here is one of those. A project that started and stopped and started and stopped until seven long years had rolled quickly past.

The project started in 1984 when Donnie was still part of the Smith Bros. and Fetrow shop on Lyndale Avenue in Minneapolis. Donnie wanted a long, narrow bike, one made almost entirely by hand, a bike that

used Harley components—heavily modified— wherever possible. With help from the crew at the shop, Donnie built a long narrow frame from scratch. His design called for shocks mounted under the transmission, an extra long swingarm, and a strong fork angle.

During the next two years, Donnie was nearly able to finish the bike. The unique rear suspension didn't work out as planned, so the bike was converted to conventional dual-shock rear suspension. After two years of work in his spare time, Donnie had a rolling chassis, but had yet to finish all the details that show up at the end of a project. He had the bike eighty percent finished and looking good when everything started to change.

The first change was at the shop. Donnie and his partners decided to close Smith Bros. and Fetrow. The market was changing. People weren't building custom Harleys. Instead they were buying Wide Glides and Softails from the factory and customizing them with a few chrome goodies. After closing the shop, Donnie bought a house, equipped a small shop, and started building bikes at home.

That extra long, extra narrow custom motorcycle was parked under a tarp, buried in the garage with about ten other bikes. Finally, in the midst of building bikes for his customers, Donnie got the bug to build one for himself.

Donnie pulled the bike out from under the tarp, rolled it into the shop and stood back for a long, hard look. A quick inventory showed a frame with swing-arm and fork, a narrow tank, and a custom rear fender with a built-in oil tank—all covered with a coat of dust and surface rust.

The first step was to do all the finish work on the frame, the rear fender, and the tank. Donnie had built the gas tank from the two halves of a Fat Bob tank and two additional, smaller tanks. He cut, sectioned, and fit pieces until he had the long, lean shape he was after. Though the shape was there, the one-piece tank had

Next page
This rear view of Donnie Smith's personal ride shows a great deal of innovation. Note the small, frenched taillight, the license plate built into the rear fender, the hand-built open primary, and the hand-built tank with the mystery gas cap opening.

9

never been finished. Donnie's brother Greg got the job of sanding and finishing the tank and fenders and molding the custom frame.

While the frame was out Donnie rounded up some of the parts needed to finish the beast. Late-model 35mm front forks were found, cut 2in, and overhauled. These later forks feature double slider bushings, meaning a fork that operates with less friction—a fork that works much better when the fork angle stretches toward fifty degrees.

At the back of the chassis Donnie ordered two new Fournales billet shock absorbers, air-adjustable for both ride and height.

The motor Donnie had planned to put in the bike was a Shovelhead. In the years between the bike's conception and completion, Harleys had changed in a

The front view shows a strong fork angle, dual four-piston front brakes, and a great paint job by Kevin Winter. Note how well the tank fits the frame—without the normal gap between the gas tank and the frame tubes.

number of ways. Chief among those changes was the overwhelming acceptance of the Evolution engine. Jim Ulasich at Eagle Engineering was picked as the man to convert the engine from a Shovelhead to an Evolution. Jim welded up the cases, moved the studs, and installed Evolution barrels and heads. While the engine was in the Eagle Engineering shop, Jim installed a Crane cam and solid lifters and tapped the new heads for a second set of spark plugs. To fire all those spark plugs, two Morris magnetos were installed.

Though the original bike would have carried a four-speed transmission, Donnie found a good five-speed transmission to mount behind the new/old engine. To connect the engine and transmission,

Next page
Nearly the entire bike was built by hand, including the open primary, the unique shift lever, the oil tank that is actually part of the rear fender, and the small air dam.

The engine in Donnie's ride is a Shovelhead bottom end mated to an Evolution top end. The heads are drilled for twin spark plugs, thus two magnetos are used to fire all those *plugs. The carburetor is from Dell'Orto, while the pipes were built by hand.*

13

Previous page
This photo shows more nice detail work. Note how the fender flares to cover the chain and how the fender strut is incorporated into the fender itself. Air-adjustable billet shocks from Fournales were painted to match the body.

Donnie bought a Karata primary belt drive. The belt primary would allow Donnie to create the open primary that was part of the original plan.

The frame and other essentials came back to the shop in primer, and Donnie and his friend, Rob Roehl, assembled the bike before sending all the parts out for final paint. At the front of the bike they bolted on the new fork and a 19in Sun rim laced to a Sifton hub. Unable to find rotors that would work with the combination of Sifton hub and Performance Machine calipers, Donnie simply made his own.

The rear rim is from Sneaker, bolted to a hand-made hub. The tire Donnie found for the rim is a monster 195/60x15in tire meant for automotive use. On the right side, Donnie and Rob bolted on a pair of Performance Machine calipers tied to two separate master cylinders.

The rear fender Donnie had built so many years before—formed by widening and trimming a FLH front fender—needed a little finishing before it could be used. Rather than bolt a big taillight on top of the fender, Donnie decided to use the slim taillight from a 1940 Chevrolet. He frenched the lens into the fender and mounted the socket assembly on the fender's backside. At the very bottom of the fender Donnie fabricated an opening just wide enough to slip in the license plate from behind.

When Donnie was sure that he had all the parts necessary for the new bike and that they fit correctly, it was time to take it all apart for painting. As Donnie always says, "The paint is what really makes a bike. If you don't get the right paint job on a bike, it doesn't matter what else has been done." Kevin Winter was chosen to paint Donnie's new ride.

The unusual and very detailed paint job took careful planning and skilled application of the House of Kolor materials. First, everything was sprayed with a base coat of platinum pearl followed by a top coat of candy red. Next, the flames were taped off in reverse—with tape actually covering each flame lick. Then a white Shimrin base was applied, followed by gold, followed by a dusting of pearl for extra sparkle. Finally, after the striping, all the parts were covered with a protective clear coat.

The finished bike contains almost too much detail to list: hand-formed tank and fenders, open primary, "flamed" solo seat, fender rails integral with the rear fender, polished and painted cylinders, the list goes on and on.

Donnie's new bike took a long time to build, but looking at the finished product, it's easy to see why. One look at this detail monster from Donnie Smith shows the finished project was, indeed, worth the wait.

A Winning Hand

It's all in how you play your cards

When Drag Specialties contracted Donnie Smith to build a bike, the task seemed simple enough. Build a high profile bike to highlight products from both the Drag Specialties and the Arlen Ness catalogs. Drag Specialties would provide the bike and Donnie would transform it from stock to stellar. Donnie could use anything he wanted from either catalog. The job seemed at first like turning a kid loose in a candy store.

It all started with a '90 Fat Boy, which belonged to sprint car and IndyCar racer Stan Fox, the brother of Fred Fox, chairman of Drag Specialties. The Fat Boy was delivered to Donnie's shop along with an open account with either Drag Specialties or Arlen Ness. Donnie could basically do as he pleased. Stan told Donnie that he wanted a modern bike, a fat bike, a pink Harley, and he wanted it all in time for Sturgis.

The first task was disassembly and cleaning. The motor was to be left stock, so Donnie shipped the motor and transmission to Mallard Teal for some hot blue urethane paint on the cases, cylinders, and the transmission case.

The big task facing Donnie was to choose the parts for Stan's new bike. Since Donnie likes his bikes to flow, this was more than just picking the neatest or the newest stuff and bolting the new parts on the bike. The job was more like designing the ultimate Fat Boy. Donnie describes the job as "putting together a winning hand from the cards I was dealt."

Donnie knew he wanted the bike low and long and just as massive as he could make it. The first modifications were made to the chassis. The front of the bike was lowered 2in with new fork springs from White Brothers. At the same time the lower fork legs were swapped for another pair with mounts for dual brake calipers. The rear end of the bike was lowered too, nearly as much as the front—again using a kit from White Brothers.

However, you can only lower a bike so much—especially a Softail—before things start to drag. In order to lower the bike farther, Donnie chose fenders that would pull the bike down visually. From the Arlen Ness catalog he ordered two Tail Dragger fenders. Tail Dragger is a good name because the back side of these massive fenders almost meets the ground. Mounted on the bike, the long tails tend to pull the entire motorcycle closer to the asphalt.

Arlen makes his fat fenders in two widths but only to fit the rear wheel. Donnie ordered two fenders, one 7in wide and one ultra-wide 8in unit. When the fenders arrived Donnie cut and trimmed the 7in fender

Next page
While many people like Harleys because they're so narrow, there is a new trend toward fat-ness. Components on this bike—from the Arlen Ness fenders to the extra-wide bars—were chosen to make the bike as fat as possible.

to make it fit the front wheel. The rear fender was smoothed and mounted to the bike with two Ness fender struts, designed to keep the fenders nice and low on the bike.

Working with the fat theme, the stock Fat Bob gas tanks were exchanged for 5gal tanks. Stan wanted a solo seat for his wide ride and Donnie scoured the catalogs for a simple, solo seat that would blend with the bike's lines. Unable to find the right seat, Donnie

helped design a prototype seat that will soon go into production.

The first seat built had too much padding in the front. Donnie tried to explain what he wanted. "You need the padding farther back where it will do you some good. I wanted the front nice and thin so the edge of the seat would match the edge of the Fat Bob tanks. That way when you look at the bike from the side there's no interruption in the line coming off the tanks and continuing to the rear fender." With the fifth mock-

The PM-Aero aluminum wheels have been painted in the same hot hue as the engine. Polished GMA rotors put the squeeze on polished, ventilated rotors.

up, Donnie finally got the seat he wanted—one that becomes part of the total motorcycle rather than just something you bolt onto the bike when everything else is finished.

With the fat Tail Dragger fenders keeping the bike close to the ground, Donnie wanted the right exhaust. Staggered duals may look great on a Sportster but this ride needed something different, something long and low. Stan wanted big "can" style mufflers for the hot rod effect, so Donnie used a Drag Specialties dual exhaust system and adapted a pair of big FLT mufflers to the exhaust pipe on either side.

A bike this big needs plenty of stopping power. The four GMA calipers were shipped to Donnie via the polishing shop. The large rotors, polished and ventilated, came from the Arlen Ness catalog. Though the catalogs were filled with calipers and rotors, there was no bracket for mounting twin calipers at the rear, forcing Donnie to manufacture a bracket of his own.

This ultimate Hog needed just a few more things to make it all come together—like a handle bar wider than the horns on a Texas Longhorn, and fat 16in rubber on both ends, spinning on super-light Performance Machine (PM) Aero wheels. None of the air dams in the catalog seemed right for the bike, so Donnie crafted one by hand.

When all the parts had finally arrived and everything had been trial fit a hundred-and-one times, there was really only one thing left. Stan wanted his new motorcycle pink, and he wanted it painted with scallops. Although Donnie likes his bikes bright, pink just didn't seem the right color for a Harley-Davidson. It was Mallard Teal who suggested hot pink in combination with deep rose and hot blue.

Mallard created the scallops in deep rose with blue accents, sprayed over the hot pink. With the blue wheels and engine cases, the paint job goes beyond bright. Electric might be a better way to describe this bike.

Stan's ultra Fat Boy was supposed to be finished in time for Sturgis, but then the whole project was also supposed to be relatively easy. Waiting for parts, adapting parts to fit, and making parts that weren't in anyone's catalog took more time than Donnie could have imagined at the start.

Even though the bike missed Sturgis, it was finished in time for the big motorcycle dealer show in Louisville, Kentucky. The Drag Specialties booth was very popular that weekend. In fact the bike was buried in a mob throughout the show. Yes, the bike took more time and more effort than expected, but with the attention it attracted at that first show, it all seemed worthwhile.

Donnie compared the project to being dealt a hand of cards. After a few good draws from the catalogs and some shrewd moves of his own, Donnie Smith came up with a royal flush.

Form vs. Function

Mechanical Engineer—or Artist?

Mechanical engineers build machines where form follows function—machines designed to perform a task. These creations state their reason for being through their shape. Artists are often accused of ignoring function by turning the form follows function criteria upside down and designing projects where beauty takes the front seat and function rides in the back of the bus.

Willie Ditz's pro-street Harley is different than most of the bikes seen at the curb. The design came about as a way to solve a problem. The fat tire and the long swingarm were designed as functional elements of a new design. The fact that this is a nearly perfect blending of form and function stands as testimony to the bike's builder, a man who is neither engineer nor artist but perhaps an intriguing blend of the two.

Willie bought the Softail late in 1984 when Softails were new. He immediately ripped it apart for a little modification. During the next five years, the bike evolved from stock to custom. The real trouble started in 1989 when Willie took the bike to Tator Gilmore.

Tator is the owner of the Chrome Horse, in Spencer, Iowa, a shop well known in the region for building killer Harley motors—drag race motors that will take a bike well into the single digits. Willie told Tator his Evolution engine was just too slow. "Like a row boat without any oars," Willie said.

So Tator went to work. He and the crew ripped the engine down to nothing and started in fresh. They kept the Harley cases and the Harley heads, but used performance aftermarket parts for almost everything else.

The flywheels and rods are from S&S, the $3^5/8$in pistons are from Axtell, contained by Hyperformance cylinders. On top of the cylinders are two Harley cylinder heads, massaged by Tator with bigger valves and ported passages. A Crane cam makes the valves go up and down, and an S.U. constant-velocity carburetor feeds gas to the monster motor.

When the new motor was installed Willie was a happy Harley rider, zooming around on his black Softail with the killer motor. There was only one problem.

Previous page
The rear tire is the largest motorcycle tire that Donnie could find: a 180/55x17in gumball from Dunlop. The taillight is part of the design for the tail section. The license plate tucks neatly in underneath.

The problem was smoke. Not engine smoke but tire smoke. The problem arose whenever Willie hit the throttle. It seems Tator had done his job too well. Even in third gear Tator's mountain motor would turn the rubber on the rear tire to jelly. Willie had a fast bike, but one that was hard to ride and even harder to launch when he took it to the drag strip.

Some riders would have just mellowed out with their right hand or detuned the motor slightly. Not Willie. Not Mr. Speed and Power. Willie had visions of a longer chassis and a wider swingarm. All in the interests of function. He wanted all this to get the bike to launch from the line, hook up correctly, and fly down the strip.

Willie had the dreams, but he needed someone to turn them into reality. He needed someone who could understand what he wanted and put the whole thing together in a package that looked as good as it ran.

Next page
Truly a monster motor, this 93ci BIG twin was built by Tator Gilmore. Using S&S flywheels and pistons, Hyperformance cylinders, and his own brand of magic on the Harley cylinder heads, Tator produced an engine that severely overpowered Willie's stock Softail chassis.

A race bike needs a large tachometer, and Willie has his set in his line of view. Not a lot of Harley engines run nearly 7000rpm. Most will do it, but only once.

29

When Willie started dreaming, the name that came to mind was Donnie Smith. Willie and Donnie have been friends for many years. Willie told Donnie about his dream bike, a Softail with enough rubber and

enough wheelbase to make good use of all that horsepower.

Donnie started on the project with a complete disassembly. The frame was left stock, except for the

---

Profile: Donnie Smith

Donnie Smith started life on Mom and Dad's farm in southern Minnesota. Though it's been some years since Donnie left the farm for the Twin Cities of Minneapolis and St. Paul, many of his strengths and habits seem to stem from that rural background.

Donnie spent part of his high school years at a special rural school. Almost like a trade school for young men and women, its emphasis was on shop classes such as engine overhaul, welding, and sheet metal fabrication. Though Donnie's first job when he hit the Cities was at Honeywell, working as a stock boy, it wasn't long before his natural bent for machines led him to the drag strip where he became part of a successful team campaigning a Willys Gasser.

Between weekend races, Donnie and his partners were fabricating parts for other racers. Soon it became a real business, named Smith Bros. and Fetrow. The shop became a way to make a living and a means of financing their own drag racing habits.

The business was originally designed to build race car parts, but a few motorcycle parts got through the door. At first they were small projects for friends. Somehow those little side jobs became more and more common until the shop turned completely to motorcycle repair and fabrication.

Smith Bros. and Fetrow was a "chopper shop," in the vernacular of the period, and a successful one. Though it seemed he was always behind the counter, Donnie found time to design and build both high profile bikes for himself and innovative products for the motorcycle aftermarket. Frames, forks, and a variety of smaller pieces were designed and manufactured by Smith Bros. and Fetrow and sold through motorcycle shops across the country. Donnie had a hand in the design of many of those parts.

When the modified motorcycle market went soft some fifteen years after opening their store, the three partners decided to change with the times and quietly closed the store.

Donnie's plan was to take some time off, maybe do some traveling, then get a job at one of the other shops in town. Looking at the wonderful designs that have come from Donnie's shop in the past year, we can all breathe a deep sigh of relief. To have Donnie Smith running the counter at another store would be like asking Richard Petty to drive a taxi, or having Willie G. design toasters. Watching him today, at work in his own little shop, it seems that this is what Donnie was meant to do, that his past experiences were training for this job.

Watching Donnie at work is always enjoyable. Here is a man doing what he likes to do, and what he's very good at doing. It doesn't hurt that Donnie is, by his own admission, "a willing talker." He has nothing

to hide. He's usually more than willing to explain what he's doing and why, how a certain piece was reshaped to better fit the lines of a particular bike, or why the swingarm on a Shovelhead was reinforced.

Donnie remembers well his days on the farm. "I remember haying with Dad. You spent the whole damned day throwing fifty and sixty pound bales of hay on the wagon. You didn't quit at 4:30, you worked until dinner time and then usually you went back out and worked another two or three hours."

There are no bales of hay in the garage, but the hours are often reminiscent of those days on the farm. When projects have to be finished, Donnie feels there's nothing to do but work. When deadlines get really tough—such as just before Sturgis—a small crew of trusted friends seems to appear as if by magic, to pitch in and help get everything done on time.

Donnie Smith seems to combine the best of rural values with his own special talent for building motorcycles. The work ethic we hear so much about is alive and well—at least in this one small shop, where it is part of the motivation that creates such great custom motorcycles.

extra rake at the steering head. The real changes to the chassis happened in the rear, where Donnie fabricated a new swingarm.

Willie wanted another 5in of swingarm. Donnie talked him down, and they settled on a 4in extension. Working with a special jig left over from the days of the Smith Bros. and Fetrow shop, Donnie cut the triangular Softail swingarm down to its very basics. When Donnie got done cutting and trimming, there was only about half the swingarm left: just the pivot point, the shock attachment point, and the lower half of the original swingarm.

Donnie used rectangular tubing to form the backbone of the new swingarm. Essentially, the tubular box sections ran from the frame pivot all the way back to the axle mounting point, much like a conventional swingarm might. The bottom of the original Softail

swingarm was welded to the bottom of the new horizontal members, creating a very strong, triangulated design. When he was finished, Donnie had a new, longer swingarm, one that retains the original Softail shock position and geometry.

The swingarm was built to accept the largest street tire Donnie could find, a 180/55x17in fatty from Dunlop. Once the swingarm was mounted on the bike and the tire and wheel mounted in the swingarm, plans could be made for the rear sheet metal.

Willie wanted to pursue the drag race look with the rear sheet metal. He didn't want a wide, round fender like the Pro Stock bikes run. Willie wanted a wide rear body section reminiscent of Top Fuel bikes.

With the wheel in the swingarm Donnie cut out a mock-up of the new flat-topped rear body section. The mock-up was only cardboard, and only in two dimen-

This long swingarm uses the bottom of the original swingarm, combined with a new horizontal member for a very strong triangulated design. The swingarm was length- *ened and widened so the rider could better use the power of the large displacement motor enhanced with the addition of NOS.*

sions, but it let Willie stand back and visualize the finished bike. He could be sure this shape was really what he had in mind. The mock-up worked for Donnie too, helping him plan the exact shape of the metal, where the taillight would mount, and how the rear body section would blend with the frame and oil tank at its forward edge.

Once the basic shape was determined, Donnie went ahead and formed the tail section from sheet metal. Most of the actual forming was done on the sheet metal brake, first one side and then the other. Each side panel was given a crease for more shape and additional strength. After the two halves of tail section were formed and trimmed, they were tack-welded together. Between the front of the tail section and the gas tank, Donnie shaped a sheet metal panel to form the seat base while at the rear he began shaping a taillight assembly.

Taillights, even on the most custom of Harleys, often end up as bolt-on items. Donnie wanted something smoother, something better integrated into the tail section itself. At the very end of the new tail section, Donnie welded a flat panel with two large slots. Red plastic would fill the slots and a light assembly would be added from the inside.

Donnie added one more thing under the new sheet metal. The 4in of additional wheelbase left a cavity under the seat. It just so happens that a bottle of ha-ha gas is about 4in in diameter. With the nitrous bottle mounted in a handmade bracket under the seat, no one had to know about Willie's laughing gas.

The rest of the body pieces came from a variety of sources. The stock gas tank was discarded in favor of a smaller Quickbob tank that was modified with the addition of a Ninja-style gas filler cap. To enhance the race-bike look, an Arlen Ness cafe fairing was bolted to the front fork.

The front fork itself was left alone. Willie had already cut the tubes 5in to get the bike nice and low. He and Donnie decided that the cut tubes and the additional fork rake would give them just the height they needed. The single front brake was deemed adequate; however, both the caliper and the rotor were sent out for polishing.

Because the new swingarm was longer than stock, the original shocks just wouldn't handle the load.

Donnie knew he needed something stronger, but how strong? The answer was a pair of air-adjustable shocks from Fournales. These air-filled shocks would allow Willie to adjust both the ride quality and height. Like the front, the stock rear caliper and rotor were given the shiny treatment and left alone.

When the tank and fairing and the Chicane wheels from Performance Machine were bolted on, everything seemed to fit. Blending the mostly round lines of the Softail with the rectangular tail section was tough to do, and was one of Donnie's worries. Yet, when all the pieces were bolted onto the bike for a final trial fit, the effect was very good. The only thing left was the paint.

Mallard Teal (no relation to the paint) is one of the Midwest's best known painters of custom cars and motorcycles. Mallard chose IROC teal blue (a GM color) and contrasting scallops in magenta candy pearl. The teal was sprayed first using PPG urethane paint. Following the taping, Mallard sprayed the magenta using a one-step candy/pearl product from the PPG paint catalog. After drying, the magenta was followed by two light clear coats. Brian Truesdell of St. Paul, Minnesota, did the fine pinstriping in a lighter shade of magenta to make each scallop stand out. Finally, the entire paint job was sprayed with another two coats of clear in order to achieve a perfectly smooth finish without any ridges caused by the different layers of paint and pinstripes.

When the parts came back from the paint shop, it was just a matter of bolting everything together—all in a mad dash to make ready for Sturgis. The faithful in Sturgis thought the bike was great. Crowds would often form to view the bike when it was parked at the curb. Editors of certain well-known magazines insisted Willie let them place scantily clad women on the bike for photo sessions. Yes, Willie likes his new Harley very much, especially the great paint job.

Not only does Willie's dream bike look good—it works! Willie reports that it rides better than it ever did stock. The extra tire and wheelbase make the monster far easier to launch. Willie can finally make use of the estimated 150 horses. It's a bike that looks as good as it works, built by a man who understands that function may be be great—but it certainly isn't everything.

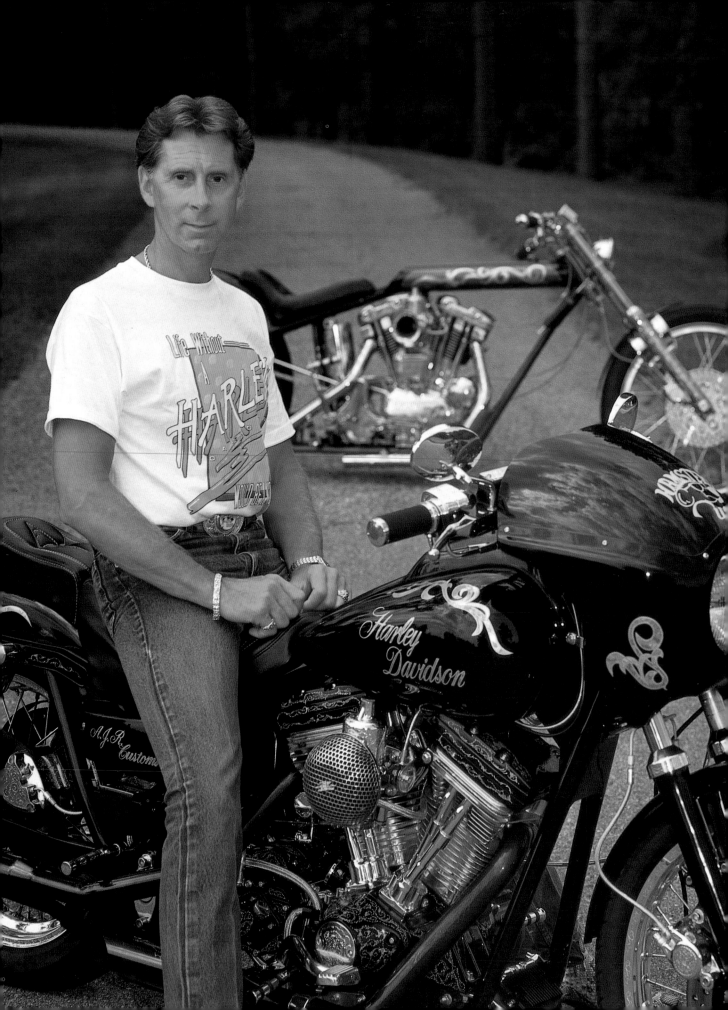

Chapter 2

Al Reichenbach

Blower Bike: Cooked up from scratch

Al's Blower bike was conceived during a trip to California to visit Arlen Ness. Al and Arlen have been friends for years, and Arlen gave Al the full tour of his shop and facilities. Among the products that Arlen pointed out during that visit, one thing that really caught Al's eye was the five-speed frame. The frame had a lot of advantages as the starting point for a new bike project. It was designed to provide the look of a four-speed or older FX frame in a package that would accept a rubber-mounted engine and five-speed transmission. Arlen's five-speed frame could be ordered with a 2in or 5in stretch, and a fork angle of thirty-three or thirty-five degrees.

When Al left California he told Arlen he needed one of those nice five-speed frames, a relatively conservative one with only 2in of stretch and a thirty-three degree fork rake. Al ordered a double-rail swingarm at the same time, then went looking for the rest of the parts needed to finish the project.

Al hates to do things halfway. He wanted a really special engine for this new bike—a blown engine. First, he called up Paul Keghal at Milwaukee Harley-

Davidson to check on the availability and cost of a new Evolution engine. Then he located a Magnuson blower and drive kit. The five-speed transmission was the last of the big items Al needed and he found one at a swap meet.

Once Al had the big parts at the shop, he put the frame on a lift and began assembling his new motorcycle. Because this was a full custom bike, Al decided to put everything together in the raw, ride the bike enough to shake out all the bugs, and then blow it all apart for plating and painting.

For wheels he chose an 18in rear and a 21in front from Akront. Chain drive was chosen for the rear wheel because it allowed the use of a larger wheel and tire, in Al's case a 160/70x18in Metzler tire could be fitted between the dual rails of the Ness swingarm. For rear shocks Al chose a pair of Harley-Davidson air-assist shocks designed for an FXRT.

The front fork Al used is a narrow-glide with caliper mounts on both lower legs. Two inches were taken out of the tubes before the fork was assembled and mounted on the bike.

Once the new machine had wheels and suspension, Al began mounting the blower and fabricating all the little brackets and parts that make up a complete motorcycle. The blower was mounted on the right side, close to the engine, driven off the left side with power transmitted and across the front of the frame through a set of pulleys.

Though the right side blower location makes for a somewhat complex drive system—most of which was built by hand—it keeps the intake tract nice and short. It's one of those trade-offs. Other blower locations make the drive system simpler but the intake tract much longer. Long intake systems involve lots of plumbing and plenty of opportunities for the air-fuel mixture to cool off. This can cause the gas to condense out of the airstream and result in a poor-running engine.

The blower was geared at ten percent overdrive, with full boost at ten pounds. With that additional cylinder pressure, Al decided to leave the Evolution

Next page
The rear wheel is an 18in model, while the front measures 21in in diameter. The bike has been lowered about 2in. Al likes to paint his own bikes, in this case with black emeron.

Al's Blower bike is based on an Arlen Ness frame, an Evolution that is force fed by a Magnuson blower engine, and a five-speed transmission.

with stock compression and mostly stock internal parts. Among the few internal modifications were an Andrews cam and adjustable pushrods. Drive between engine and transmission was through a Primo belt instead of a chain. The belt primary allowed an open primary without any lubrication—a necessity considering the addition of another belt and pulley to drive the blower.

Once the blower and drive were sorted out Al fabricated his own gas tank based on an aftermarket tank. When Al had finished, there wasn't much of that tank left. In order to make it sit nice and low the tunnel was moved up. At the same time the tank was sectioned along each side, and additional metal was added to make the tank longer and thinner. As if that wasn't enough work, Al also fabricated a flat bottom.

The other body parts were a little easier to come by. The fenders, cafe fairing, and oil tank are from the Arlen Ness catalog.

For brakes Al chose twin Harley calipers squeezing ventilated rotors in front, and in back a two-piston Performance Machine caliper mated to another drilled rotor. The balance of the small brackets and parts—bits like the chain guard—are more of Al's creations.

It was winter when all the pieces and parts finally fit as planned. The Wisconsin weather was pretty chilly, but Al didn't care. During the week between Christmas and New Year's he put more than 100 miles on the bike. He started the new year right, by putting the bike back on the lift and ripping it apart.

Chassis and engine parts were sent to the powder-coating operation while the rest of the parts were prepped for paint in Al's shop. The shakedown rides had gone pretty well. Just a few things needed changes—the height of the rear fender, for example, and the taillight mounting.

The engine and blower worked great, though it seemed pretty lean on the top end. After talking with

The engraving here is a fine filigree of designs and patterns. Even the belt guard for the blower drive is covered in the fine scrollwork.

other people with blower bikes, he called Rivera and ordered a special needle for the S.U. carburetor, one designed for turbo and supercharger applications.

When all the parts came back from powder coating and engraving it took one week of marathon work sessions to put the bike together. When it was finished, Al had done it again—created another unique and functional motorcycle. He now had a bike built to look—and run—unlike any other.

A Touch of Class

A bike that stands alone

When Al Reichenbach built this black and gold beauty, he wanted a dependable bike, one he could ride long distances with plenty of comfort. The FXR model with its rubber-mounted engine and relatively long suspension travel seemed like a logical starting point for the new road bike. Small, Arlen Ness-type fairings were becoming popular at this time, so Al decided to try the new look and take a little wind off his chest to boot.

The starting point for the new project was an FXRP, a low-mileage police model that Al was able to acquire from the Milwaukee factory after they were

Note the intricate patterns on the S.U. carburetor. Al had to find a special needle for the carb—one designed for

supercharged applications—in order to get a mixture rich enough on the top end.

through using it as a test bike. Al wanted a color scheme that would make the bike stand out without being totally outrageous. He wanted a bike that looked good while keeping its composure—a bike with a lot of class. He chose black, with gold used as an accent. Instead of chrome, the new bike would have gold on many engine and chassis parts. The final touch would be the engraving, a feature on most of the bikes Al builds.

Al sent the engine cases, chassis parts, and frame out to a powder-coating operation. The powder coating would provide a good finish for the parts, yet allow them to be engraved. Powder coating is like painting without liquid. Think of a spray of finely ground paint particles being shot at a swingarm or engine case. The attraction between the powdered paint and the part being painted is generated with D.C. electricity—much the way chrome or gold plate is applied. In addition to creating a surface that can be engraved, the powder coating is more durable than a conventional painted case or swingarm. These powder-coated surfaces are much less likely to be chipped by rocks or nicked during assembly.

The gold part of the color combination came from the real McCoy: twenty-four carat gold plate. Al shipped the rims, cylinders, heads, shock springs, and a variety of smaller parts to Brown's Plating.

While subcontractors were busy putting the correct black or gold on the engine, chassis, and accessory parts, Al prepped everything else for a complete

Powder-coated parts—like the engine cases and rocker covers—offer a good surface for engraving. Engraved gold and black parts and the gold leaf on the tank and fenders all work well together.

Profile: Al Reichenbach

Al Reichenbach is a quiet man, the kind of man you have to get to know a little before he opens up. Al has a lot to say—it's just that you just might have to wait awhile before he gets around to saying it. Dressed in blue jeans, cowboy boots, and a T-shirt, Al looks like any other Harley enthusiast you might meet along the street. The only difference is in the details. Al's jeans fit just right, his T-shirt is squeaky clean, and the boots aren't made out of just any old cowhide.

Al is a neat man, and that neatness translates from his personal habits to the bikes he builds. The bikes are always clean, even if Al just came back from a ride. The paint is nice, the details are well executed; and no expense is spared in building them just right. If the gold-plated bolts Al needs for an FXR project cost more than most riders would spend on a paint job, it's okay because Al will settle for nothing less than perfection.

Al grew up in Black River Falls, Wisconsin, where his father owned a farm implement store. Repairing the John Deere combines in Dad's store was the beginning of Al's mechanical education. A few years after high school Al moved to Janesville, Wisconsin, where he got a job with a construction crew. While working construction, Al applied for work at the GM plant. Before long the people at GM called and told Al to come to work, and he has been working at the GM plant ever since.

Not long after getting the job at GM, Al bought a motorcycle, a nice, clean Triumph. That Triumph was followed by a series of bikes, and in time Al acquired an old Sportster. The Sportster had been neglected by its owner, and Al started its restoration by adding a new rear fender, a Cobra seat, and a fresh paint job. Al's knack for buying and selling meant that before the Sportster was down the road, there was another Harley parked in the garage. It got to be a habit. Al would buy a bike, fix it up a little and ride it until someone made him an offer he couldn't refuse.

At first he just cleaned up each bike, added a few trinkets, and maybe repainted the sheet metal. But as time went on, the bikes got wilder and wilder. Al remembers that when his favorite painter got sick, "well, I went out and bought a spray gun and an air compressor and set up an area to paint in my garage. I just started doing all my own paint work. After a couple of years, I was doing paint jobs for other people, candy paint jobs and flames and all the rest."

Like a snowball rolling downhill, Al's Harley habit picked up momentum as Al acquired more bikes and more skills. In the late 1970s, he started selling parts out of his house. When the demand was large enough, Al decided it was time to open a real store.

At the time, Al was still gainfully employed at GM. Al remembers thinking, "I was eating off of GM, so I figured I didn't have to make a lot of money at the store, just enough to pay the overhead and some extra." In addition to running his store and working full time at the GM plant, Al was still building bikes. That big snowball was rolling faster and faster and the bikes were getting more and more radical.

From warmed-up stockers, Al's bikes had evolved to full-on customs. His first radical bike was a Sportster engine in a long Arlen Ness frame. After that, Al bought a wrecked Shovelhead cheap and transformed it into a radical custom. He was developing a reputation and wasn't at all popular with other bike builders on the show circuit. When Al took one of his bikes to a show, he usually took home both the bike and the trophy. Al's attention to detail, his insistence that everything be perfect, the neatness, and the lovely paint were the characteristics that created a long string of winners.

He still owns the store, an old three-bay gas station painted orange and black with Harley logos on the walls. Inside is a parts counter, a remarkable amount of parts, and a large shop.

The number of radical bikes coming out of Al's shop has slowed down in recent years. Good help is hard to find, and Al often ends up alone at the shop, trying to keep up by working both before and after his shift at the plant. The end is in sight however. In just a few years Al can retire from GM, and that liberation will allow more time for the shop and more time to build custom motorcycles.

Until then Al keeps putting in those long hours that might wear out anyone else. And when time permits, he can sneak back into the shop to work on and plan another wild Harley-Davidson. But don't hold your breath waiting for Al's latest project—because Al won't roll out his new bike until everything is just perfect.

Al's FXR started out as the police model. The success of Al's design is due to careful refinement and an unusual color scheme.

paint job. Al likes to do his own paint work, so he painted the tank, fenders, and smaller parts himself.

After he finished the paint work, Al sent the parts out for gold lettering and trim. More than just a matter of painting the gold onto the black, application of gold leaf requires a special set of skills. The letters or scrollwork must be cut out of large sheets of gold leaf. Then the sizing, the special adhesive used with gold leaf, is applied to the gas tank or fender. Finally, the letters or scrollwork are pressed onto the sizing.

In Al's case, the lettering was done by the late Wes Stockman and the true gold leaf was applied by Bob Rollins. Wes used a straight gold leaf for the letters while the rest of the patterns were applied using variegated gold leaf.

Following the Midas touch of the two artists, Al sprayed all the parts with a clear coat for protection and to create a smooth surface.

Reassembly couldn't start until the primary cover, rear sprocket, engine cases, and rocker covers were sent out again, this time to John Bittner for engraving. Al felt that engraving helps to add detail to a bike without bolting unnecessary stuff on the outside of the machine.

The assembly didn't take long once all the parts were arranged in one place. Al wanted his bike lower,

The Harley-Davidson script is done in gold leaf and covered in multiple coats of clear for protection.

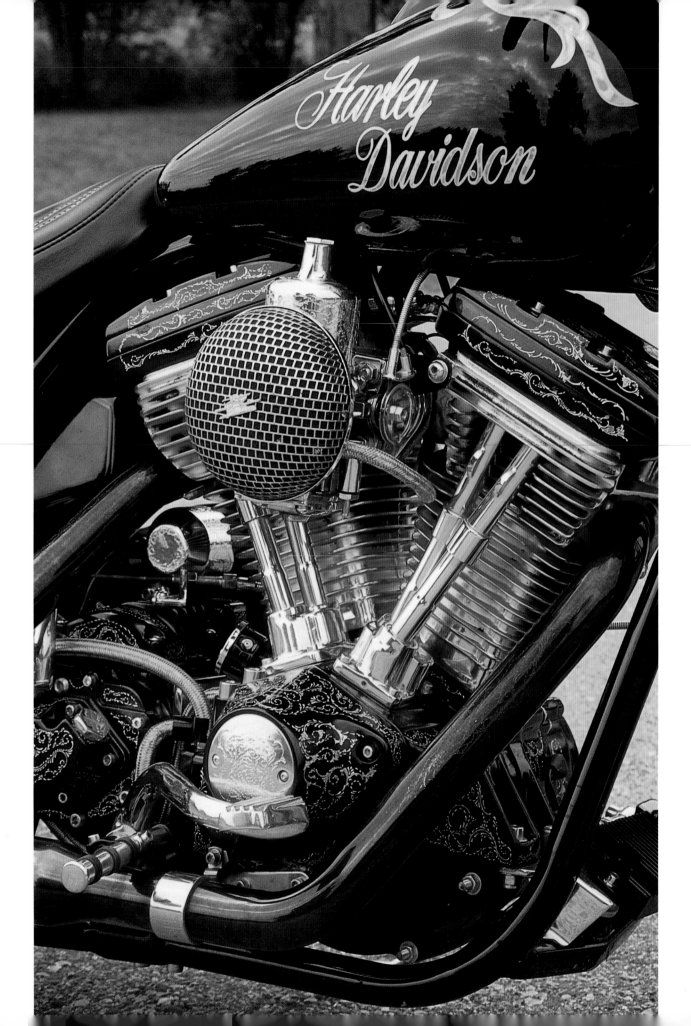

but not so low it would drag in the corners. Two inches seemed like a good compromise, which is how much Al took out of the fork tubes before putting the fork back together. The rear of the bike was lowered a similar amount by first extending the end of the swingarm and then locating the lower shock mount out on the end of the arm.

The new FXR came together piece by piece. Gold-plated calipers were bolted to powder-coated fork legs and the small handcrafted chain guard was attached to the swingarm with gold-plated bolts.

The engine Al set in the frame is nearly stock; a Screamin' Eagle cam was the only internal modification. Externally, it's a different story, of course. The cases are powder coated and engraved, as is the transmission. The barrels, pushrod tubes, heads, and parts of the S.U. carburetor glow with that precious shine. Even the oil lines are a gold braid. Black pipes from Cycle Shack exit the heads, mounted to the engine with gold-plated clamps.

At a time when paint jobs get wilder year by year, Al's gold-plated Harley Davidson doesn't even try to compete. Though the fads in paint go from flames to scallops, from reds and yellows to neon green, the gold-trimmed FXR stands apart—timeless and in a class by itself.

Looking Back

A two-wheeled history lesson

When it comes to customized motorcycles, most of us want to know what's new. What is the fastest, sexiest, and most modern creation to come from Arlen Ness, Donnie Smith, or any of a number of Harley builders? In our headlong scramble into the future we sometimes forget from where we came. With the current interest in custom Harleys, it might be instructive to look back at one particular show-winning custom Sportster from Al Reichenbach.

Al's Sportster was built in the early 1980s, a time when the Sportster was king and radical custom meant just that—radical. The trend was moving away from long springer forks toward shorter and more functional front suspensions.

Al admits to being very impressed with the bikes Arlen Ness was building during that time. Known as Diggers or Street Diggers, these long, lean bikes borrowed heavily from the drag strip look with their exaggerated length, solo seats, and hard-tail frames.

By this time, Al had been into custom Harleys for more than ten years. He was accustomed to winning when he took his bikes to the shows, shows like the

Custom Bike Show at the Hilton or Holiday Inn Surfside hotel during Daytona Bike Week. In 1982 he won the Big Twin Class at the Hilton. For 1983 he wanted to do something different, something more difficult. Al wanted to win the radical class, and he planned to do it with a Sportster.

The bare beginnings of Al's new ride consisted of a Sportster engine stashed away in the shop. The frame for the new showstopper came from C.C.W. with an 8in stretch and a forty degree fork angle. Al removed the top tube and installed a larger tube in its place. This larger tube would function as the gas tank—another idea borrowed from the drag race bikes. Al capped the tube at either end with small concave covers, tapped it for a gas spigot, and welded on a threaded section for the gas cap.

At the back of the frame Al started with a Digger fender and then added side panels of his own design. Each panel was louvered and welded into place. To give the assembly enough strength, a small diameter piece of rod was bent up and welded to the outer edge of the fender and side panels. When the welding was finished, Al molded the edges and rough areas. The fender blends so well with the rest of the frame that it truly seems the frame might have come that way from the factory.

The front fork is from a Sportster, trimmed 2in in length, chrome plated, and engraved. The dual disc brake calipers are Harley factory units, plated in gold with rotors plated in chrome. Twin fork dampers act both to avoid the shakes at high speeds and as fork stops on either side.

The engine in this long Sportster is meant as much for showing as for going. Most visible are the barrels. The lower fins are gone altogether, while the remaining fins have been ground to a hex shape and then gold plated. Most of the engine and its accessories are gold dipped. Chrome is used sparingly—primarily on the cases and exhaust pipes—and serves as contrast to the abundant gold.

Al knew it would take more than gold and glitter to win the radical class. He needed just the right paint and accents. Starting with a paint gun filled with lacquer from the House of Kolor, Al sprayed a multiple base coat that started at the bottom of the bike as a silver, blended first to a gold and then to a black pearl. Over the blended base coats, Al sprayed a candy-brandywine. The blended base coats created a color change from the bottom frame rails to the top of the fender and gas tank—from a bright brandywine with a lot of red in it to a black pearl that looks almost black.

Yes, this story has a happy ending. Al did win the show and took home the trophy as Best in the Radical

Previous page
The large rear tire, minimal fender, and gas tank integral with the frame are all part of the look. The bike appears functional despite all the gold and glitter.

Class. After the show Al put the bike on display at a few of the Harley dealerships, then took it home, where it rests today. Though it may not be the newest or the fastest, the Sportster is a nice bike to keep around because you can't really know where you're going unless you know where you've been.

Next page
This is one of those bikes where the closer you look, the more you see—and what you see is detail and more detail. The scrollwork looks like what you might see painted on the ceiling of an old theater or cathedral.

Much of the old Sportster engine is gold plated, as is the oil tank and rear master cylinder. Al did the lovely paint job with acrylic lacquer—beginning with a multicolored basecoat followed by a top coat of candy brandywine accented by gold leaf.

The Sporty engine shows a lot of nice detail, like the gold-plated magneto housing and the engraved exhaust pipes.

Note, too, the concave caps used to create the gas tank/top tube.

Chapter 3

Arlen and Cory Ness

Ferrari Bike: Wildest, Fastest, Most

Arlen Ness has built many a custom motorcycle and won many an award for Best of Show, Best Paint, or Best in Class. Yet, among the hundreds of bikes that Arlen has built, one stands tall above the rest. That one bike is the red monster Ferrari bike. This is a bike with more of everything. More horsepower, rear tire, details, engine, blowers, and NOS bottles than any other two bikes combined.

Arlen's projects don't start in the shop, they start in his head. This new bike started as Arlen's desire to create something special—something special even for Arlen Ness. A bike that would make a bold statement about Arlen and his skills.

The idea called for a massive rear tire, enormous engine, and full body work. With these ideas rattling around in his head, Arlen consulted the late Jim Davis for help in designing and building the frame. He and Jim decided that it should be a hardtail frame in order to avoid the complexity and cost of a swingarm frame. The hardtail design would also make it easier to enclose the entire bike in body work. There would be

no need to leave room for the rear wheel to move within the body work.

Arlen's search for a monster motor led him to buy John Harmon engine cases, barrels, and heads. The goal of the Harmon engine is cubic inches. The Harmon cases accept standard Harley flywheels and bottom end parts. The special cylinders take a piston that measures 4¼in across, designed for a big-block Chevy V-8. Arlen had the motor set up with standard Harley flywheels for a total of 128 stump-pulling cubic inches. (Imagine the kind of cubes that are available by combining the big jugs with a stroker kit.)

On top of those enormous cylinders are two of John Harmon's special heads; the intake valves have a diameter of 2⅛in and the combustion chamber is drilled for twin spark plugs. Those big valves are actuated by a Crane cam and the mixture is fired by an Accel ignition system.

Arlen thought the big pistons and valves were a good start for a killer motor, but only a start. Each cylinder has its own Magnuson blower. Each blower is fed by two Dell'Orto carburetors. Arlen wasn't sure this combination would produce enough power, so for those situations when he needed just that little extra, he had two nitrous bottles installed—one for each cylinder.

The transmission for the new bike had to be a five speed, belted to the engine with an 11mm Primo belt. Arlen wanted belt drive to the rear wheel, too, but wasn't sure one belt would do the job. From the five-speed transmission power runs through a short chain to the jackshaft. The jackshaft, mounted behind the transmission, has a belt sprocket on both ends. Final drive to the rear wheel is by twin belts, one on each side of the wheel.

Arlen wanted to ensure that no one doubted who built this bike. When Steve at Pacific Broach made the jackshaft assembly and the belt sprockets, he worked an Arlen Ness *A* into the milling pattern.

The rear wheel itself is a two-part racing rim, wide enough for a 265/60x16in tire. (By comparison, a new

Next page
This rear view shows off the lovely body panels pounded from aluminum sheet by Craig Naff at Boyd Coddington's shop. Testarossa-like side scoops feed air to twin oil coolers. Exhaust pipes exit the body work like a Formula 1 bike.

mounted four-piston brake calipers and stainless rotors inside the rim, inboard from the drive sprockets.

While Darrell was machining center hubs and spokes for the rear, he also made a matching system for the front wheel. The front brake calipers are a bit

Testarossa carries 255/50x16in tires in the rear.) The center hub is a custom piece machined from solid aluminum by Darrell Hayes. Between the hub and rim are spokes shaped like an Arlen Ness A. Darrell also

Profile: Arlen Ness

Among Harley builders, one man is better known than any other. One name is recognized the world over as the best known of all the bike builders. That man, that name, is Arlen Ness. After almost thirty years of building custom motorcycles, Arlen Ness has reached the top.

Getting to the top wasn't easy, especially climbing there the old-fashioned way—with lots of sweat and hard work. Yet, Arlen climbed the stairs one custom Harley at a time. Each one was different from the one before, most of them winners, all of them created in the mind of a very talented designer.

Arlen's first experimenting and customizing was done on cars, his own cars, his friends' cars, repainted, modified, and improved. Motorcycles, however, had always held a special allure for Arlen, and finally the attraction was simply too much. The first thing Arlen had to learn when he brought home that old Knucklehead was how to ride. Shortly after learning how to ride, he pulled his new bike apart for his first motorcycle paint job. The paint job won Arlen a lot of attention on the street, and soon people were asking him if he could do a "nice paint job like that for my bike."

Arlen quickly graduated from simple paint jobs to elaborate paint work combined with long, stretched tanks, custom fenders, and handlebars of his own design. In fact, Arlen's Ramhorn handlebars were his first big commercial success. Arlen remembers twenty years ago, "I worked a day job and only opened that little shop of ours in the evenings. Those handlebars were great. For a while there were people waiting everyday when I opened the store, just to buy a pair of those bars."

The Ramhorn bars were only the first in a long string of great Arlen Ness designs. Inspired by the drag racers, Arlen started building bikes with long, angular tanks. Arlen, and the other aftermarket companies, sold a lot of those tanks. Arlen's designs have followed phases in his bike building: supercharger phases followed by a turbocharger period followed by more blowers. Arlen has a knack for taking a big piece like a blower—one with a lot of visual appeal—and integrating it into the total design for the bike. The result is a machine almost larger than life.

Arlen has come a long way from that first Knucklehead and first tiny store. The Knucklehead now sits in the Oakland museum. Arlen's current store is large, with separate mail order and service departments in addition to the standard retail counters.

It would seem that Arlen has it made, but in reality each success brings with it added responsibilities. Each new product brings pressure for another, each year's travel schedule is more hectic than the previous year's. Arlen's escape valve is an event like Sturgis or Daytona, when business demands are reduced and there are days when the only thing on the schedule is the day's ride to Sundance, Wyoming.

It all started thirty years ago with a love of motorcycles. Today, sitting astride one of his bikes in Sturgis, waiting for the line of bikes to leave on a run, you can see that same young man. Though there are a few lines in his face, the spark in Arlen's eyes as he looks over the bikes is the same. At heart, Arlen Ness is still just a kid, fascinated with those two-wheeled machines.

Previous page
Front view shows bodywork that flows from the headlight to the rear fender. Front fork turns within the bodywork to provide a clean, unbroken line. Red paint was mixed up from special pigments by Jon Kosmoski at the House of Kolor.

unusual, designed and built by Darrell. Each caliper carries four pistons, is integrated into the fender brace, and squeezes brake rotors that are bolted to the inside of the rim. Of course Arlen's name appears on each front rotor.

When Jim Davis asked about a fork, Arlen dropped off one from Simons, built in an upside down fashion, and a set of custom triple clamps from Darrell Hayes.

As the frame and engine for the new bike neared completion, Arlen had to consider the body work. Arlen had recently finished a car project that would impact the new motorcycle. That project was the customizing of Arlen's Ferrari 308 by Boyd Coddington's shop in Los Angeles. The sketches had been done by automotive designer Thom Taylor. When Thom finished the drawings and Craig Naff from Boyd's shop finished the metal work, Arlen's Ferrari bore a certain resemblance to a new Testarossa. Because the Ferrari project had been such a success, Arlen naturally turned to the same team for help with the body work on the new scooter.

Based on Arlen's ideas, Thom Taylor worked up a series of rough sketches. Arlen picked out the drawings with lines similar to his Ferrari, and Thom worked up a second, more accurate set of drawings.

Next, the almost finished frame and engine were shipped to Boyd Coddington's shop where Craig Naff, Boyd's master metal man, made a set of cardboard mock-ups based on Thom's drawings. The mock-ups allowed Arlen to step back and visualize what the bike was going to look like in the flesh.

During the next three months, Craig took the bike from cardboard mock-ups to finished, hand-formed aluminum panels. The panels were so clean and the lines so nice that once Arlen got the bike home and finished the mechanical details, he started riding it in aluminum—without paint, without any body filler.

The shakedown ride lasted an entire season. Finally satisfied that the big beast was as rideable as it was unique, Arlen pulled the entire thing apart for the final painting and plating. The red color was specially mixed by Jon Kosmoski as a special favor to Arlen. Dennis Dardanelli applied the red paint and did the gold leaf work on the headlight housing.

The final effect is almost larger than life. The front view emphasizes the mechanical side of the bike, with the multiple carbs, chrome blowers, and manifolding dominating the view. From the back, the super-fat rear tire is the first thing to grab the viewer's eye. The tire is bigger than anyone would conceive could be bolted into a motorcycle.

In typical Arlen Ness fashion, the total effect is more than just the sum of its parts. Two blowers, two NOS bottles, and more horsepower than a 5.0 liter fuel-injected Mustang are all somehow blended into a package that not only pleases the eye, but goes down the road as well.

Too much motorcycle. This bike will stand as the ultimate in radical custom Harleys for many years to come.

Forward into the Past

A bad case of nostalgia-*ness*

Arlen Ness has a reputation for building great custom motorcycles—cutting-edge bikes that utilize the latest in technology, bikes that set new trends in customizing. Arlen is a man moving forward, aggressively pushing the edge of the envelope, always busting out of the old ways and ushering in the new.

So when Arlen decided to go back, to create a nostalgia Panhead, he naturally did it with a unique flair. The bike Arlen built is a singular blend of old and new.

The basic style of the bike, with its Panhead engine, hardtail frame, springer fork, Fat Bob tanks, and tall bars is certainly a well-known look. The application of that look, however, is all new.

Arlen based his new project on an aftermarket hardtail frame—a simple frame without any extra stretch or rake. This frame would provide the stubby look reminiscent of the earliest choppers. The front fork is a polished springer from the folks at Paughco spinning a 21in Metzler tire. The rear hoop is of the traditional 16in spoked variety with another Metzler tire.

The preferred engine for an early chopper was the Panhead. Arlen was able to find enough parts at home and in the shop to assemble a clean Pan. Before the reassembly was complete, the cases and cylinders were sent out for polishing to ensure the engine would look as good as it ran.

With the traditional frame, forks and engine, Arlen had the parts needed to assemble a "correct" old Panhead. However, being Arlen Ness, that wasn't quite enough. Arlen wanted a bike that represented more than mere nostalgia.

Arlen's break from the old started with the gas tanks. Yes, they are Fat Bob tanks, but they have been narrowed, eliminating some of their fatness and changing the look of the bike slightly. The rear fender (*there ain't no front fender*) is a fiberglass Tail Dragger from Arlen's own catalog, and it reaches almost to the asphalt.

Splashed across those narrow-bobs and that fat rear fender are some of the wildest flames ever seen on a motorcycle. The orange and lime green pigments were specially mixed by Jon Kosmoski of the House of Kolor. Arlen started with a base coat of bright orange. Next, he taped off and painted the ghost flames, then covered everything with a coat of pearl. After another long session of taping, Arlen sprayed the lime green flames and had them striped by Ron Morrelli.

Not content with a flamed paint job, Arlen wanted a truly flamed motorcycle. On the left side, the four-speed transmission and Panhead engine are connected by a Primo 3in belt. The belt drive allows the use of an open primary, made up of a chrome enclosure with an embossed flame pattern as an integral part of the cover. On the right side, a matching, flamed air cleaner makes it look as though the engine has backfired and spit flames all along the side of the bike.

Next page
Arlen's chopper starts with all the right stuff—things like a springer fork, hardtail frame, and Panhead engine—combined with a wild paint job.

Profile: Cory Ness

One might imagine the son of Arlen Ness growing up drinking his milk from an inverted Harley piston, or that he would be predestined to follow in his father's footsteps, customizing first his tricycles and then his fat-fendered Schwinn bicycles.

It wasn't that way for Cory Ness. In grade school and high school Cory showed more interest in basketball than in anything with two wheels. Arlen remembers that sometimes Cory would come out to the garage and help a little with a project, but only sometimes. Early in high school, Cory accompanied Arlen to some of the shows, always in the role of spectator rather than participant.

Cory made his turn toward two wheels when the kid across the street wrecked his Honda dirt bike. Cory, in early high school at the time, came to Arlen and explained that the bike could be bought for just a few bucks. His idea was to fix it up and then sell it. Arlen gave his consent and soon the little Honda was spread across the garage floor. With a little help from Dad, Cory fixed up the Honda and sold it for a tidy profit.

Cory's next project was a Sportster. Though he still didn't have a license, Cory built a clean, contemporary custom Sportster. One of the magazines picked up on the bike and ran a feature. As soon as Cory got a license, he started riding the Sportster to school. The die was cast, Cory had been bit by the motorcycle bug. One custom bike followed another. Cory soon started showing his bikes. After coming close to winning on the ISCA show circuit, he built *Risky Business,* a bike built to show. He took his new bike to shows all over the country by himself and took top motorcycle honors that year.

Cory's first motorcycle project, the little Honda, showed not only a certain ability for motorcycle building but also Cory's talent for business. To this day, Cory doesn't keep his bikes very long. Once built, the challenge is over, Cory sells the bikes and moves on to another. His bent for business has proved an asset to Arlen as the business has grown from a small motorcycle shop to a multifaceted operation with worldwide sales.

As the business grew, Cory developed into the manager of the entire Arlen Ness store. The mail-order, retail, and service departments are all Cory's responsibility. Arlen credits Cory with the accelerated growth the store has experienced in the past few years. Overseas sales, symbolic of the growth, now account for twenty-five percent of their sales.

Each year, the store grows, and each year Cory's responsibilities grow as well. Yet, Cory manages to build one or two bikes each year. Cory's bikes are always modern, always a little different from anything Arlen might build. What he shares with his father is a good sense of design and proportion. Though he likes them stretched out, Cory's bikes are never too long and the parts work together to form a whole motorcycle.

Cory's sense of design puts him in a good position to contribute to the ever-growing list of products in the Arlen Ness catalog. Their new flamed accessories—flamed derby and points covers, with the flamed pattern milled into the cover itself—are one of Cory's ideas.

A man with more than one skill, Cory is an experienced motorcycle builder with a knack for business—good credentials to have as Arlen Ness Enterprises and the custom Harley market roll rapidly into the 1990s.

Previous page
A rear view shows off the Tail Dragger fender, ventilated chain guard, and unique primary "un"-cover.

The hardware and accessories are an interesting mix of old and new. The front brakes are twin discs with polished calipers and rotors, and the rear brake is a disc as well. The handlebars are tall—that is, high. Yes, high bars, often known as ape-hangers, bolt directly to the front fork uprights.

The shifter is a Jockey shift arrangement, though Arlen remembers firsthand the troubles created by foot clutch operation. For those times when the rider needs both feet on the ground, Arlen installed a clutch handle

Next page
The rear fender is fiberglass, known as a Tail Dragger. Note the nice arch in the fender supports. Upswept pipes and off-set taillight bracket are more of the right stuff, while the disc brake is very current.

A Panhead is the only logical choice as the powerplant for a retro-chopper. This one has been completely rebuilt and carries the latest cylinder heads with better oiling charac-teristics. Air cleaner is exactly the kind of far out, one-off, creative mad-ness that has made Arlen famous.

No one can accuse Arlen of being in a rut. Orange with green isn't a garden-variety color combination. Arlen did all the elaborate taping and spraying himself—including the subtle ghost flames.

on the left bar so the clutch can be operated by foot or by hand.

The final effect is a motorcycle with enormous appeal. It is a bike that works on more than one level. For some, the Panhead opens windows to their younger, wilder, and perhaps more carefree days. For others, the Panhead is simply a great motorcycle—a wonderful blending of old and new. It is a bike that goes forward and back at the same time.

Wheeling into the Nineties

Putting your best wheel forward

Cory Ness likes his bikes a little longer than most. Stretched-out Harleys with fat rear tires, or modern bikes that reach into the future but are still grounded in good old hot rod tradition are his style.

Cory's FXR with the wild paint and directional wheels started life as a new FXRT with extra touring paraphernalia. Cory rode it in full trim for a short time before realizing he needed a new ride for Sturgis. The idea of riding a fully laden touring rig during the week of Sturgis—while everyone else rode stripped and souped little bar bikes—didn't have much appeal. The solution was obvious: transform the FXR from massive to mini. The only complication was time. It was already late June when Cory made the decision, with Sturgis a little more than a month away.

The first part of the project was simple. It is a process that motorcycle customizers and builders have been practicing since the very beginning of time: Cory stripped the bike of all its extra "stuff." He took off the bags, fairing, and fenders. In fact, Cory stripped the FXR right down to a frame and engine—then he cut off the front of the frame.

Because the FXR was nearly new, Cory planned to sell the parts he stripped off and use the money to help build the new bike. Cory remembers, "Because the bike was almost brand new, I had no trouble selling all the parts. I even sold the front frame section."

With the front of the frame missing, the first step in the reassembly was a new front section. Cory had one fabricated with an extra 5in of stretch and a fork angle of about thirty-eight degrees. From that new frame section hung a wide-glide fork, trimmed 2in and mounted with a pair of Ness triple trees.

The frame section gave the bike the long look Cory was after, but the bike needed more. The answer was the wheels. Cory started with a pair of solid aluminum wheels from Rev Tech. The front is a 21in rim (replacing the stock 19in), while the rear rim is a wide rim designed to accept a 170/70x18in Metzler tire. The solid wheels were worked over on a computerized milling machine using Cory's design. The net result is a super-wide, ultra-modern wheel, one that contributes a great deal to the overall look of the motorcycle.

Putting a fat rear tire on an FXR requires more than just a wide rim. It also requires converting the bike to chain drive to eliminate interference problems between the tire and belt. In Cory's case that still wasn't enough because the tire rubbed between the two top frame rails, necessitating a widening operation at the back of the frame.

To cover that big rear tire and provide the modern look Cory wanted, a Streamliner fender from the Ness catalog was used. The slim front fender is theirs too—a Ness Sport fender. Slowing down all this modern machinery are JayBrake four-piston calipers at both the front and the rear, squeezing large-diameter polished rotors.

Rounding out the bike is an assortment of the latest, sexiest hardware Cory could find. The grips, levers, and mirrors are all part of the Ness-Tech series. The points and derby cover are part of the rotational covers offered in the catalog, and they work in harmony with the unique directional wheels.

The engine for Cory's latest scooter is a relatively mild Evolution motor. The tight timetable meant that any modifications should be those that are easily made with the engine in the frame. Cory started with the carburetor, one of the new Series E shorties from S&S. In order to open the stock valves a little farther and for a little longer, a Crane cam and adjustable pushrods were installed. Finally, to ensure that the exhaust exits the cylinder (so more fresh gas can get in) a two-into-one flared exhaust pipe was added. The final touch for the engine was the chrome S&S air cleaner.

The wild paint job started with black applied to the tank and side covers by Cory, using urethane from the House of Kolor. When the black had dried, the parts were taken to Jeff McCann who added the wild blue panels with orange waves. When the tank and side covers and fenders were finally delivered, Cory could put it all together and take that first shakedown cruise, with just days to spare before packing for South Dakota.

The new bike looks good from almost any angle. From the rear the fat tire and wild paint dominate. From the side, the long profile makes the bike appear stretched out and ready to run. The spinning wheels make it look as though it's always in motion, breaking new ground for Cory Ness.

Previous page
A derby cover carries a directional pattern that works well with the wheels. Although it came with a belt, Cory's ride has been converted to chain drive, allowing more room for the big back tire. The black paint is Cory's, and the graphics are by Jeff McCann.

The rear fender is a Streamliner model mounted to the bike with special polished fender struts.

This big twin carries some extra polishing outside. Inside a Crane cam and pushrods give a little extra lift to the stock valves. An S&S Shorty carb feeds the fuel into the engine, two-into-one pipes help get it out.

Chapter 4

Dave Perewitz

Re-'NEW': There just isn't anything like a new motorcycle

1982 was a good year for Ed Jamerson. In the spring of that year, Ed brought home a brand new Harley, an FXWG. With the extended fork, bobbed fender, 21in and 16in wheels, Ed's Wide Glide was the ticket to ride. And ride he did. For eight great years, Ed rolled the highways of Connecticut and the surrounding eastern states.

During those years of riding Ed met a lot of other Harley riders. One of those riders was Dave Perewitz, owner of a shop called Cycle Fab in Brockton, Massachusetts. Ed always admired the bikes that came out of Cycle Fab, so when his trusty Wide Glide finally showed serious signs of wear and tear, Ed knew there was only one place to take his trusty steed.

Dave Perewitz was put in charge of rebuilding and modernizing Ed's fine old Harley. Dave explains, "Ed is a little bit conservative. He wanted us to completely go through the bike, but he didn't want it to look too wild. He wanted it lowered, blacked out, and he wanted more power than it had before."

Getting Ed more power was done through a complete rebuild, including new S&S pistons and flywheels with stock displacement, and an Andrews Model B cam with Andrews adjustable pushrods. The Shovelheads were turned over to Terry Goldman for a good valve job and a little work on the ports. When the final engine assembly was done, the old points-style ignition went in the trash can. Instead, Dave installed a new electronic ignition from Dyna. In order to get enough fuel to the motor, an S&S model B carburetor was bolted in place with an Arlen Ness two-into-one pipe to get everything out again.

The stock four-speed transmission had all those miles on it, too. Dave thought they should open it up and check everything out. Ed thought as long as they were in there they should go all the way and install a set of Andrews close-ratio gears.

Giving the bike a more aggressive and modern stance was achieved by raking the fork neck an extra eight degrees. In addition to raking the fork, the tubes were trimmed 2in to help lower the bike. Dave ordered lower fork legs from Frank's with mounts for dual front brake calipers, then sent them out for powder coating in shiny black. The frame itself was simply painted black with urethane paint.

At the rear, Dave moved the lower shock mount farther back to drop the bike, then sent the modified swingarm out for chrome plating. Ed and Dave had decided to use limited chrome plate on the bike, so the

Next page
This black Shovelhead was built in 1982 and updated for the nineties. Many of the original parts—like the gas tank—have been exchanged for more modern pieces.

Previous page
This Shovelhead engine has been modernized, too, with a complete rebuild, an Andrews cam, and an S&S carb. Black wrinkle paint on the cylinders is the same paint used at the factory.

19in front rim and the 18in rear rim both went to the powder-coating shop along with the lower legs and the hubs.

The gas tank on Ed's new ride is a Quickbob tank with an added feature. In order to provide more detail and make the tank appear more like a true set of Fat Bobs, Dave ran a bead right up the center of the tank with the welder. Then the bead was smoothed and molded before the tank was painted.

Next page
Trimmed tubes in front and relocated lower shock mounts in the rear help get the old Shovelhead closer to the concrete. A Corbin-style seat and raked fork help to stretch the bike out and enhance the low look. Note the chrome-plated swingarm and chrome derby in a black primary cover.

A Performance Machine master cylinder with the logo milled into the cover is a good example of the modernizing that was done to this Shovelhead.

The lower legs and rims have been powder coated to create a super-durable surface. Front brake calipers are from Brembo, while the small air dam came from Don Hotop's shop in downtown Fort Madison.

The paint job for the bike is basic black. Dave painted the tank and fenders in black lacquer and then applied a clear coat. The same black powder coat used on the lower legs was used on the rims and the hubs as well. In order to keep the bike from being too black, Keith Hanson added purple and blue highlights and a set of pinstripes to the fenders and the new gas tank.

Ed Jamerson didn't ride his new bike to Sturgis. He made arrangements with Dave to ship his bike to Sturgis so he could fly in and meet Dave there. The

Profile: Dave Perewitz

Dave Perewitz is the man behind Cycle Fabrications, a custom bike shop in Brockton, Massachusetts. Watching Dave at an event, with his happy-go-lucky attitude, a nice Harley to ride, and good chums to ride with, it's easy to think he's got it made—that this ability to build bikes and make a living at it came easily. In reality, Dave acquired his skills and experience over a lifetime of bike building.

Dave's very first vehicle was an old car. He describes it as "just something to tear apart and put back together again." But the first motorcycle wasn't far behind. Dave's first two-wheeler was a stock 1964 Sportster, purchased when he was sixteen years old.

During his high school years, Dave started hanging around a local body shop. Before long, he was "one of the guys," helping out with sanding and simple paint jobs. The body shop was his introduction to the world of body and paint work. Dave's first motorcycle paint job was applied to a certain Sportster, and before long he was painting motorcycles for other people as well.

About high school, Dave says he "never learned a thing until senior year." That was the year he took machine shop class. After graduating, he worked first as a machinist and then as a mechanic at the local Chevy garage. In his free time, he fixed motorcycles in his home shop.

By the early 1970s, motorcycle repair and fabrication became more than just a part-time occupation. Dave put up a small shop behind his father's house with a small spray booth and a separate assembly area. This was the beginning. Three years later, Dave opened a separate small retail store to sell parts and accessories.

Dave is quick to point out a couple of key people who helped out in the early days. First was his brother Donnie. As Dave got busier with his little business, Donnie did all the machine work on custom and billet parts. When Dave opened the retail store, Donnie took responsibility for the shop, leaving his brother to concentrate on the new store and building the bikes.

The other leg up came from Arlen Ness. Dave remembers, "I met Arlen in about 1975. Arlen really helped. He helped me with the business side of it, and he introduced me to some other bike builders and people in the business. Arlen gave me a real push."

With hard work and a little help from his friends, Dave moved into a larger shop in 1980. A few years later they moved into a new store as well. Though the new store has both a retail and a shop area, Dave still builds most of his bikes at the separate shop—the one managed by his brother Donnie.

Some bike builders work from a sketch. For Dave, the ideas and concepts go from his head to his hands. Whether it's a turnkey Softail or a flamed paint job, he just jumps into the project and does it. Although this spontaneity may not work for everyone, Dave's results certainly speak for themselves.

He is proud of his crew and often brags that they can "do it all." At the retail store they sell parts and accessories, and offer installation of the parts. At the shop, Dave is free to design, build and paint motorcycles. Though the business is much bigger now than in the early days, he doesn't want it to get too big, not to the point where there are too many employees and too much turnover.

Dave likes the advantages of a small crew. "The nice thing about the crew we've got now is the fact that everybody gets along. There aren't a lot of arguments and all that. We're just big enough. We can do everything, from selling the job to machining the special parts to painting the bike. We almost never have to farm work out and wait. It gives us a real advantage."

So while Dave may not "have it made," he says that he's doing all right. "I'm doing what I want to do, I'm paying my bills, and I'm having fun at it. There aren't that many of us doing what I do, so I feel pretty lucky to be where I am."

Previous page
Chipped paint of the old gas station contrasts with the recently built FXR with its fresh candy red paint job.

truth is, Ed had never seen the finished bike until he saw it sitting in the parking lot at the motel in Sturgis.

It was like that first experience in 1982 all over again. Ed Jamerson had another new bike—only this one was better than new—and Ed had a whole week with nothing to do but ride, mother, ride.

One That Got Away

The good ones are hard to hang onto

Professional bike builders seem to have trouble keeping a bike in the stable for themselves. It's kind of like the shoemaker's children who go to school barefoot. Dave Perewitz seems to have that problem in spades. Whenever he builds a great bike, like the twin carburetor bike, somebody comes along and makes Dave an offer he can't refuse.

When the twin carbs bike was sold, Dave got busy in his shop until suddenly it was early summer and he had nothing to ride. The answer was a certain FXR that Dave brought back from the swap meet earlier in the back of his pickup truck. This particular FXR was rough, very rough. An early Shovelhead FXR, the parts

Next page
The early model FXRs used the Shovelhead engine—this one has been rebuilt using S&S components, a valve job with some porting work, and an S.U. constant-velocity carburetor.

Dave painted the side panels on the gas tank in neon red, then asked Ron Mason to create the logo and do the pinstriping.

Previous page
The left side shows limited chrome—just a few things like the
coil cover, shift lever, and pegs. Note the molded frame and
how well the side covers fit at each corner.

were all there, but everything on the bike needed serious attention.

The plan for the FXR was simple: build a basic custom bike, one that could be assembled without tying up the guys in the shop. At the same time, this would be Dave's personal bike so it would have to exhibit Dave's particular style.

Dave likes his bikes with a lot of fork rake, so modification of the old FXR started at the front of the frame. Dave dialed in an additional ten degrees of rake. To help get the bike in the weeds, the upper shock mounts were moved forward and then the frame welds were smoothed and molded.

The engine in this swap meet special was plenty tired. The old Shovelhead would need more than a top-end job in order to run well. Following an inspection, Dave decided to bore out the Harley cylinders .010 and install new S&S pistons with a modest 8.5:1 compression ratio. The bottom end was replaced, too, with new flywheels from S&S in stock dimensions. The

The dual disc brakes are from Harley-Davidson. The Progressive springs drop the front about 3in. The lower legs are painted with black urethane paint.

camshaft Dave chose is a modest grind from Andrews, their model B, connected to stock lifters and adjustable pushrods. The heads were sent to Terry Goldman for a three-angle valve job and some porting work.

Before the engine was reassembled, Dave took the time to paint nearly everything black. In order to make sure the engine paint would stand up to heat, solvents, and rock chips, Dave filled the paint gun with urethane. The cylinders were painted with genuine Harley-Davidson wrinkle paint, the same paint they use at the factory. Because of the extreme heat, it's hard to get paint to stick to the heads, so they were left their natural color.

Once the engine and frame were reassembled, it was time to paint the bike and get it ready for its inaugural run in South Dakota. The brightness of the red paint job was created by the white pearl base under the candy red lacquer. When he finished the paint job, Dave created the panels on the tank with a neon red. Ron Mason painted the unusual Harley logo and did the pinstriping on the tank, side covers, and air dam. The side covers are from Arlen Ness, while the small air dam is from Don Hotop.

The rest of the bike was assembled using a mixture of aftermarket and genuine Harley parts. The fork legs came from Frank's Forks. The tubes are uncut, although the progressive springs drop the front of the bike about 3in. The calipers, both front and rear, are the Genuine Harley units, painted in black urethane, squeezing polished rotors. The carb is an S.U. with a simple mesh filter. The nice, megaphone exhaust pipes—the ones without a baffle—were built by Brad Lovely and chrome plated by Atlantic Coat Plating. Dave figured that if the bright red paint didn't get everyone's attention, the *loud* exhaust certainly would.

Though Dave's plan wasn't radical, the bike worked well. When Dave took it to Sturgis, the old FXR attracted a lot of attention. One of the people who noticed the bike was Mike Kline from California. Mike wouldn't say whether it was the exhaust or the paint that grabbed his attention. Whatever it was must have been good, because the bike never went back East. Instead it went home to California with its new owner, which left Dave with a smile on his face and no shoes on his feet.

A Special Piece

One that Dave will always remember

Dave Perewitz has been in the bike building business for a long time. During that time he has built a lot of custom Harleys. Among those bikes, he has a few favorites. One of those, the bike that he calls "one of my best pieces," is the long flamed Harley with the two carburetors.

Putting two carbs on a Big Twin isn't an easy thing to do. Dave thought it would help this particular bike stand out. Like his other bikes, Dave designed this machine inside his head, without any sketches. The idea called for a fully customized Harley with a sexy, curvaceous tank, and a special engine.

The engine part of the equation was taken to Wayne Loftain. Dave and Wayne discussed how they might build an Evolution engine with two carburetors, one on each side of the engine. The stock engine, with the two intake ports facing each other across the narrow V, wouldn't allow the adaptation of two carbs, each fed by its own intake manifold. Wayne suggested that they use two front cylinder heads. By putting a front cylinder on the rear, each cylinder could be fed by its own carb, and each carb could be on a different side of the bike.

At first the idea seems too good to be true—and it is. Wayne's concept required a great deal of modification and machining to apply to Dave's engine. First, when a front cylinder is mounted on the rear, the pushrod angles are wrong and the pushrod tubes no longer fit. Worse, a stock cam won't work because the hybrid setup effectively swaps the pushrods for the new rear cylinder. The pushrod for the intake valve connects to the cam lobe meant to open the exhaust valve. If that weren't enough, the exhaust pipe for the new rear cylinder exits in the V, leaving very little room for an intake manifold from the front cylinder.

Wayne solved the problems one at a time, and he did it so well the engine looks as though it came from Milwaukee with the twin carburetor setup.

Correcting the pushrod angle problem was solved by filling and then machining new ports on the bottom of the new head where the pushrod tubes enter. In order to make the valves open in the correct sequence, Gordon Kately ground a special cam—one with the lobes for the rear cylinder switched—just for Dave's engine.

Making room to run an intake manifold to the front cylinder was almost as much work as making the pushrod tubes fit the rear cylinder. Both front and rear intake ports on Evolution engines are set slightly toward the right side. Some people have mounted the carbs or blower on the left side, but it makes for less than ideal intake and intake port shape. In figuring out how to put one carb on the left side, Wayne had the added problem of clearance between the exhaust pipe and the new intake port.

The solution involved welding shut most of the intake port for the front cylinder, then machining a new one farther to the left side. When the new intake port was finished, the heads were sent to Jim Thompson for flow bench work. Wayne wanted the heads to flow equal amounts of air—equal but superior to what a normal head would flow.

The final assembly of the new engine with two carbs was done by Cris Barbari using a set of Delcron

Next page
Dave's Special Piece is based on an Arlen Ness five-speed frame mated to a very sleek gas tank and a most unusual Revolution motor.

Previous page
The left side of most Harley engines is a pretty dull place—not so with Dave's Revolution engine with its twin carburetors.

cases and S&S flywheels and pistons. The S&S stroker flywheels brought the engine to 89ci. Wayne suggested Dell'Orto single-throat carbs, bolted to hand-built intake plumbing. Spark is provided by a Morris magneto. The unusual exhaust system was fabricated by Rich Sansone.

Dave's design for a special bike called for more than just a unique engine. An Arlen Ness five-speed, rubber-mount frame would provide a comfortable ride, one that sat nice and low. To really make it work though, Dave wanted a long gas tank, one that would follow the lines of the frame and curve gracefully over the Evolution heads.

The origin of this long tank was a swap meet special that Dave turned over to Rich Sansone. Rich carefully added metal here, trimmed it there, and then flattened the bottom of the one-piece tank.

When the tank was finished, Dave could start to paint and assemble this two-carb, two-year project.

Next page
Note the one-off, side-by-side exhaust pipes and the unusual carburetor location. The rest of the bike is strictly modern with its dual Performance Machine brakes and ventilated rotors, the strong fork angle, and the fat 160/70x16in rear tire.

Dave has been painting motorcycles for more years than he cares to admit—and it shows in these hot flames. In fact, both of these flame jobs are Dave's.

Following a coat of primer, Dave painted everything with a base coat of black followed by multiple coats of cherry kandy from the House of Kolor. Dave designed the flames to follow the contours of the tank, fading from yellow through orange and finally red, outlined in blue by Roy Mason.

The final assembly was done using a Kosman rear wheel wide enough for a 160/70x16in tire with chain drive from wheel to the transmission. The fat rubber necessitated widening the rear fender almost 2in. The fender is supported by custom struts fabricated from tubing by Dave and his brother Donnie. Brakes on the rear are a pair of Performance Machine four-piston calipers squeezing a single polished rotor. The swingarm is a dual-rail design from Arlen Ness.

The solo seat design is Dave's own, upholstered in black by Danny Gray in sunny California. The front wheel measures 18in and is mounted to a Harley fork set at a thirty-eight degree fork angle. The twin calipers are from Performance Machine, as are the polished rotors. The trim front fender is set close to the tire and carries the same great flames as the gas tank.

When Dave had finished the bike, he discovered that it worked every bit as well as it looked. The twin carbs and all the careful porting work made it a strong runner. Dave also discovered that the bike drew a lot of attention. So much attention in fact that it passed out of Dave's hands to a fella named Will Claypool. Though the bike is gone, when you ask Dave about all the bikes he's built, he'll probably tell you about this one, this one really special piece.

Chapter 5

Bob Bauder and Pete Chapouris

HogZZilla: The impossible dream

Performing an impossible task—like building two *HogZZilla* bikes in less than sixty days—is possible only by assigning the task to the right *team* of craftsmen. They must be people who are not only skilled as individuals, but who have the ability to complement one another's strengths.

Sometimes four people can do the work of five or six because they work together so well. It's that old concept of synergy: two plus two equals five. In the case of *HogZZilla*, the fab four primary craftsmen were Pete Chapouris, Bob Bauder, Larry Erickson, and Steve Davis. These four were aided by other craftsmen and by a second group that can only be called movers and shakers.

It was early January when all the major players finally got together at the shop of Bob Bauder and Pete Chapouris. They would have done it sooner but they had to wait for the bikes to arrive. The men who attended that first meeting read like a *Who's Who,* but not necessarily a *Who's Who* of custom motorcycling.

In one corner was Larry Erickson, designer of *CadZZilla*—the '48 Cadillac built for Billy Gibbons of ZZ Top fame. Larry brought full-size, full-color renderings of what the new *HogZZilla* bikes would look like. With Larry came Jack Chisenhall. Jack is a native Texan, well known in the street rod industry (owner of Vintage Air), and the man who originally brought together Larry Erickson and Billy Gibbons. Billy Gibbons couldn't make the meeting since his responsibilities with ZZ Top tend to keep him busy.

Talking with Bob Bauder and Pete Chapouris was Steve Davis, one of the fab four craftsmen with primary responsibility for the creation of the *HogZZilla* bikes. Better known for his street rod and drag racing work, Steve Davis represented the metal working part of the team. It would be Steve's responsibility to create the panels, tanks, and fenders that would shape *HogZZilla.*

The idea behind that first meeting was to critique the renderings and create a plan for the actual construction of the two bikes. The team went over the renderings inch by inch, discussing not only the overall shape, but more importantly, the team's ability to actually create those curves and panels.

As the metal master, Steve Davis' input was critical. Steve remembers the meeting as "a chance to discuss what could and couldn't be built. We softened some of the complicated corners just to make them easier to fabricate. Bob and Jack wanted some changes to the shape of the front fender. In the end the design

Next page
Soft light shows off the perfectly smooth body panel curves in a sea of harsh angles—all crafted by hand by Steve Davis. HogZZillas were designed and built to resemble the looks and lines of CadZZilla.

Previous page
The body panels were built by hand. The mechanical pieces are genuine Harley-Davidson. The rear fender is made up of three panels on each side. The tailpipe covers were some of the hardest panels to shape and the only ones that contain any filler.

dimensional Harley, these templates helped the team visualize and further evaluate the final shape of the bikes.

After that meeting, the team members and their helpers all went into overdrive, working twelve and

wasn't altered too much. The changes were more an evolutionary thing."

When the team agreed on how the bikes should actually look, Larry Erickson cut out full-size templates of the bikes from foam-core board. Like a two-

Next page
This front fender was formed from two halves with a welded seam down the middle. The unique gas tank is actually a series of panels that enclose a smaller tank. The back of the bike was lowered to get the correct fade-away-at-the-rear look shared with CadZZilla.

ZZ Top and Harley-Davidson share the billing on these bikes. Handlebar controls had to be the real McCoy, just like all the other mechanical parts. These are older Sportster units.

fourteen hours a day to build the bikes in time to lead the Bike Week parade in Daytona Beach. Considering that the project was first conceived some two years earlier, it seems ironic that the team ended up with less than sixty days to do the actual building and fabrication.

Pete Chapouris and Billy Gibbons had been friends for years. They had discussed the creation of a very special motorcycle at least two years before work began on the *HogZZilla* bikes. The project was side-tracked again and again until finally *CadZZilla* created the spark that re-ignited the bike building project.

The exhaust pipes, too, are hand-built. Steve Davis describes them as a series of large radius bends. These gradual bends complement the shape and overall look of the bikes. The air cleaner is incorporated into the chrome spear on the right *side. Its switches are hidden in the left-side spear. The spears were built from sheet steel. Everything else was formed from aluminum.*

The idea was simple enough: build two escort bikes for the Cadillac, designed by Larry Erickson, to match the lines and the look of *CadZZilla*. The final push needed to take the bike project from idea to reality occurred one day when Billy Gibbons ran into Willie G. and Bill Davidson. The three quickly determined that the bikes definitely should be built and that they absolutely had to be Harleys.

It's a long way from Milwaukee, Wisconsin, to Crestline, California, and it took longer than planned for the two new Harleys to arrive. When the two bikes arrived they were new Fat Boys rather than the Softail Customs that Bob and Pete had requested. At the risk of looking a gift horse in the mouth, Bob called Bill Davidson to explain that the Fat Boys carried the Wide Glide fork, and wouldn't work with the design they had for the gas tank and headlight housing. The dilemma was resolved when Bill called back and promised to send a pair of new Showa forks intended for the 1992 Dyna Glides.

Once the new forks were on their way and the first meeting of all the principals had been held, the actual building could begin. Having two bikes to work on proved a real boon to the project; one bike was immediately shipped to Steve Davis' shop. Two bikes meant each shop had a bike around which to form components and panels. While Bob and Pete worked at the mechanical changes, Steve began fabricating the panels and fenders for the bikes.

Steve chose to build the body panels from sheet aluminum rather than steel. The sheets Steve ordered were 3003-H14 aluminum. Each sheet was 0.063in thick—about a sixteen gauge—the same material used to build a Ferrari fender. With one of the stripped bikes at his shop and the two-dimensional cutouts, Steve went to work creating the many panels required for each fender or gas tank.

The front fenders are made up of two halves, with an invisible, welded seam running down the center. Steve formed the two halves of the front fenders and the other panels on his old Yoder brand power hammer. While the other panels were formed by eye, using the cutout as a guide, Steve built a buck from plywood as an aid in creating the front fenders. The two hand-built fenders had to be exactly the same. The metal was still formed on the power hammer; the buck was simply used to check the shape as the fenders were hammered out.

Though the team members had considered a one-piece headlight housing and gas tank, the realities of the project dictated a two-piece design. Rather than create a gas tank from scratch—a tall order—Steve used a small gas tank and crafted four panels to enclose the tank completely and provide the shape called for in the design.

The most complex part of the body work, the rear fender, was crafted from six individual panels. Each side has an upper and lower panel and then a separate panel that contains the crease running diagonally across each panel. Cynics might figure that those hand-built panels—smooth as a baby's bottom—are coated with filler. Cynics don't understand true craftsmanship.

Steve explains that the panels are metal finished without the need for any filler. Each panel is carefully shaped, then welded to the next; the welded area is passed back through the power hammer. The result of all this hammering and a little final metal finishing is an invisible seam. The minute amount of filler used on the bikes is found on the tailpipe housings, necessitated mostly by the tight time schedule.

While Steve and his helpers slaved away with the power hammer, Bob and Pete were working on the mechanical changes. In order to lower the bikes at the back, their Softail struts were replaced with solid struts that made these a pair of hardtail/Softails. The hardtail design made it easier keep the bikes low and keep the sheet metal wrapped close to the rear tire.

The new front forks were modified to drop the front of the bike slightly and mounted to the Fat Boy frames. The back was dropped more than the front to achieve that tail-dragger fade-away look called for by Larry's design. Bob and Pete had to be careful in making their mechanical changes since the plan dictated that all mechanical components used on the bikes be genuine Harley-Davidson.

Near the end of the project, sleep became a thing of the past for all four team members and the painters as well. Steve Davis is lavish in his praise for John Carambia and Tim Beard. "John and Tim did a great paint job, and they had less than two days for the whole thing. It was great they could do it so quickly because it gave us more time to do the metal work."

Pete Chapouris remembers the intense excitement of those last two days. "You know, if any one person had screwed up or just gotten sick or cut their hand badly, it wouldn't have happened."

But happen it did. The two *HogZZilla* bikes led the kickoff parade at the start of Bike Week in Daytona Beach.

The *HogZZillas* are more than just two custom Harleys. They are the impossible dream turned reality at the hands of a very special team of craftsmen.

Chopped Surprise

Getting more than you bargained for

Near the end of the *HogZZilla* death march, Bob Bauder realized he was going to sunny Florida with the two ZZ Top bikes, but *he* didn't have anything to ride. Jerry Moreland, a good customer and friend of Bob's, had left his Springer Softail at the shop. Bob knew he

Next page
A raked fork gives the Softail some extra length. Articulating fender linkage allowed Bob and Pete to get the front fender closer to the tire. The rear fender is mounted to the swingarm and moves with it over bumps. The seat is a simple two-piece design.

Previous page
These classic gas pumps make a good backdrop for an old chopper-style Softail. The Chopper theme is created with just a few key elements—the bobbed fender, small sissy bar, and ape-hanger bars.

Small, early-style taillights are mounted to the sissy bar. A bobbed fender was crafted from a Fat Boy front fender turned around, trimmed, and reshaped. Drag pipes look right at home here.

Profile: Bob Bauder and Pete Chapouris

Syntassein is the name of the relatively new partnership formed by Bob Bauder and Pete Chapouris. *Syntassein* is a Greek word, based on the root *synergos*—which means "arranging together." It's the same root used in more familiar words like *synthesis* and *synergy,* meaning the creation of something new, the genesis of something exciting. Implied in the meaning is the concept of harmony, a bringing together of things that were meant to be together, forming new compounds and concepts that end up being greater than the sum of their parts.

Automotive enthusiasts are likely to be familiar with Bob and Pete. Both are well known in the world of street rodding and automotive fabrication. Anyone who doubts their motorcycle pedigree, however, has only to look as far as the *HogZZilla* bikes to realize that these two men deserve a place in the hallowed halls of professional motorcycle builders.

The name of their corporation seems especially appropriate after talking with these two men for an hour or so. Each man is quick to compliment the other and explain how they have different strengths and how neither of them could do projects like *HogZZilla* without the help of the other. If ever two individuals were meant to be partners, Bob Bauder and Pete Chapouris were.

Pete is the former owner of the legendary Pete & Jake's street rod operation. In late 1986 that business was sold, and Pete cast about for something to do. Being too young and having too much energy for retirement, Pete ended up as vice president of marketing for the Specialty Equipment Market Association (SEMA).

During a recent lunch, Pete explained how the move from fabrication to management nearly cost him his sanity. "At Pete & Jake's, as the business grew, I went from hands-on fabrication to the management side of it. Then, during the years that I spent as v.p. at SEMA, it was a desk job again. One afternoon, I'd just really had it with the corporate thing and I called Bob right out of the blue and I said, 'Bob, I need a job. I need to come up in the mountains.' Bob didn't even hesitate. He just said, 'Sure, come on up.'" (Bob lives two hours and several light years away from L.A. in Crestline, California).

Pete started out four days a week with Bob, working in the shop, staying with Bob at his house, and going home on weekends. Shortly after beginning this new relationship, the *HogZZilla* project was born and Pete was thrown into full-time motorcycle fabrication.

Pete's motorcycle experiences started on dirt bikes. It was a means of relaxation and a way to get away from street rods. Soon, some of his friends started buying Harleys. Shortly after that, Pete started "cutting up the frames, raking the forks, modifying the tanks so they sat lower on the bike. Pretty soon I had a Harley of my own."

Bob Bauder

Pete Chapouris

Pete thinks there are many good things about his teaming up with Bob. "Bob is better at the management end that I am. He's real good with the customers. It's been really great for me to be 'hands-on' again. My old welding and fabrication skills are coming back. I'm really much happier doing it this way."

Bob Bauder, the man doing the managing, the man with the easy laugh who answers the phone, started out riding Sportsters in his home state of Pennsylvania. Bob Bauder moved to northern California in 1964, expecting to see plenty of hot rods and Harleys. He found the hot rods but darned few Harley-Davidsons, until he met a biker shortly after moving west.

"I met this Hells Angel and he explained that they had just outlawed ape-hangers and how everybody was putting on extended front ends and drag bars with risers to get around the law. Well, I had this new Sportster, and pretty soon I had an extended front end on it. Before long I was building bikes for other guys."

Two serious bike accidents and a move to the automotive capital of Los Angeles nearly brought an end to Bob's bike building. In L.A., Bob met Boyd Coddington and started building cars with Boyd in the small shop behind Boyd's house. By the early 1980s, Bob had worked with and for all the big street rod shops in the L.A. area. It was time for a change and another move, this time to the small mountain community of Crestline.

With five acres, a house for the family and a shop just down the hill, Bob started doing street rod and muscle car projects. In 1987, he built his first Softail for a customer. Soon there were more and more bike projects in the shop. It grew slowly until Pete came along and they built the *HogZZilla* bikes. The current shop load is half car projects and half motorcycle projects.

That fifty-fifty split is likely to change in the future. The Harley work will likely take up nearly all the shop's time and energy. It seems that with the success of the ZZ Top project, Bob and Pete are getting calls from all over the country. They're getting calls from people with fat checkbooks who want someone to build them a killer Harley. Another thing pushing the car projects into the corners of the shop is a rapidly evolving relationship with Custom Chrome.

Custom Chrome, one of the largest manufacturers of aftermarket parts for Harley-Davidsons, doesn't do all its product development in-house. Bob and Pete, along with Rick Doss, do a great deal of product development for Custom Chrome. Pete points to this part of the business as another case where together he and Bob can offer Custom Chrome more than either could alone.

Pete goes on to explain, "Bob has a lot more motorcycle experience than I do, so that once we have an idea, like a fender or a light assembly. I rely on his ideas for the shape of the part."

Bob picks up the conversation at this point and adds, "Once we have a shape, we make a prototype, and from that we rely on Pete's manufacturing experience from his days at Pete & Jake's. Pete is able to determine how hard the part will be to manufacture, what the cost of tooling will be, and what the gross margins will be. When we walk into Custom Chrome with a new part, it isn't just an idea for a fender, it's a whole program from beginning to end. They can just take it and run. We've done most of the homework for them."

While the Syntassein corporation might be new (their actual day-to-day business is done under the banner Hot Rods and Harleys), and the two individuals might not be old-timers in the world of motorcycle building and fabrication, no one should underestimate this pair. Together they have over fifty years of experience designing and fabricating vehicles and parts for vehicles. That experience, combined with the momentum of the *HogZZilla* project means this is a pair to watch. There is talk of a new full-bodied bike and more new products for Custom Chrome. Together, there doesn't seem to be much that these two can't do.

---

could take Jerry's Springer to Daytona and use it for the week, but somehow a stock bike didn't seem adequate for the Daytona festivities—especially after working on *HogZZilla* for more than a month.

The answer seemed obvious. Bob called Jerry Moreland and asked if he could make a few "improvements" to his Springer. Jerry figured Bob wanted to change the handle bars and maybe add some pinstripes. Jerry agreed and told Bob, "You go ahead and make a few changes and then surprise me when you get down to Daytona with the bike."

The deadline for the *HogZZillas* made it tough to find time to work on the bike. Bob realized he needed to get maximum impact from some simple changes, changes that wouldn't take too darned much time.

The inspiration for the chopper theme with the bobbed fender came when Bob spied a stock Fat Boy fender left over from one of the *HogZZilla* bikes laying in the corner of the shop. He turned the fender around so it faced backward and held it next to the existing Harley fender. From the side view the new fender looked like a good candidate for a chopper-style bobbed fender.

Bob soon had the Fat Boy fender trimmed, flattened, and reshaped. Instead of mounting the fender high enough for the tire to move under it, Bob mounted

Next page
Sitting at the gas pump in the early evening light, Jerry's chopper looks ready to cruise the local watering holes.

This engine is stock, and paint job is black with two-color scallops. The whole bike is a case of getting maximum impact from minimum input.

The frame has been molded to eliminate rough welds and the concave sections under the seat. The Harley rear fender has been narrowed, trimmed, and lowered on the bike.

the fender to the swingarm so the fender moves with the rear tire. To support the fender at the back edge, a small sissy bar was crafted.

Once the fender was mounted, Bob needed a new seat. Actually, Bob needed more than a seat, he needed a new design. A conventional one-piece seat wouldn't work now that the rear fender moved with the wheel. The answer was a hinged, or two-piece seat. The

pillion is mounted to the rear fender while the seat pad bolts to the frame. Bob reports that "the pillion thumps your backside a little as you go over bumps. At first it seems strange but after about five minutes you don't even notice it anymore."

The other major change to the bike happened at the front, where the steering head angle was changed to add another seven degrees of rake to the front fork. The stock front fender, sitting high off the tire, didn't seem right to Bob either. He and Pete talked it over and soon designed a linkage that allowed the fender to be mounted close to the tire, to maintain that tire-to-fender distance as the fork moved through its full travel.

Like the chopper bike, this Softail gets the front fender down low through the use of linkage. The rest of this bike is very *different from the chopper bike and involved a great deal more work.*

Since a chopper needs high bars, Bob ordered a pair of ape-hangers from Custom Chrome, along with the necessary cables and hoses needed to make everything work with the higher bars. The other thing a chopper needs is noise, provided by the mandatory drag pipes.

Getting everything else done took Bob longer than he had thought. He was left with only two days in which to do the paint job. Black with scallops seemed simple enough. Until it was finished, though, Bob felt the bike "needed something more." So the night before loading the truck for Florida, Bob added the purple scallops. Why purple? "We used the purple because it was the best color we had in the building at the time."

When Bob and Pete and the bikes arrived at Daytona, Jerry Moreland came over to the truck, looked everything over and then asked Bob, "Where's that Springer you said you were going to bring down?" Bob just smiled and pointed to the chopper with the bobbed fender and the wild paint. Jerry nearly fell over as he realized that the purple and silver scalloped Easy Rider bike was his.

Bob had to remind Jerry that he gave him the okay to change the bike and even suggested that Bob "surprise" him in Daytona. Well, Jerry got more than he bargained for—more bike and more surprise.

Sophisticated Softail

A lot of changes—all done in the best of taste

When Bob Bauder built the little chopper-style bike, it was a case of getting a lot of effect from a minimal amount of work. The red Springer seen here is the other, more common kind of bike. A tremendous amount of work was performed on this bike, yet the work is so subtle that it remains invisible to most people who view the bike.

The differences in the two bikes are even more surprising considering that both started out as Springer Softails and both belong to the same man, Jerry Moreland.

If the chopper bike was banged together out of necessity, the red Softail was carefully planned and thoughtfully executed. The changes to the red Softail took a full eight months to complete.

Jerry wanted his Softail with plenty of power, so Bob pulled out the Evolution V-twin and sent it to Rick Rogers. Rick believes that old adage that there's no substitute for cubic inches. Inside the engine Rick used S&S flywheels to create a 98ci stroker. On the outside, Rick had everything polished and then bolted on an S&S carburetor and air cleaner and a set of drag pipes.

While Rick was toiling away with the engine, Bob and his partner Pete were working at creating a more sophisticated Softail. In order to stretch the bike out, the fork angle was increased an additional six degrees. During the frame work, the welds were all molded smooth, including the normally concave section under

the frame—an area that was smoothed and filled until it was perfectly flat. At the rear, the bike was dropped just over 1in by installing a lowering kit of their own manufacture. The rest of the chassis is close to stock. The brakes feature Harley calipers squeezing polished rotors from Custom Chrome.

Bob and Pete lavished the greatest share of attention on the fenders and gas tanks even though the changes aren't readily apparent. The craftsmanship and the wonderful way all the seams are made to disappear make it easy to believe that Bob and Pete have spent a lot of time building street rods and custom cars.

The Fat Bob tanks were pulled off the bike and welded together into one unit. Next, the dash was welded to the tanks and the seams were filled. In place of a stock dash, Pete carved a new dash face from billet aluminum. The tanks and billet dash turned out so well that they became part of the product development program that Bob and Pete maintain with Custom Chrome. The new aluminum dash has no ignition switch; it's been moved and incorporated into the coil cover.

In order to smooth out the lines, Bob wanted the rear fender lower and closer to the tire. First, the fender was sectioned to make it shorter. Next it was narrowed to fit between the sides of the swingarm. The final touch is the nifty little taillight—actually a marker light from a Chevrolet—mounted flush under the lip at the back of the fender. The remanufactured fender wouldn't mount with stock fender rails, so a new set of rails was ordered from Custom Chrome.

The front fender was lowered, too, with linkage similar to the linkage used on the chopper bike. The articulating fender linkage keeps the fender-to-tire distance uniform as the tire moves up and down over bumps. Bob and Pete made another minor change to the front end that results in a major change to the way the bike looks. That change is in the position of the headlight, which is moved down because it's mounted to the front shock absorber.

The last step, of course, is the Kandy Cherry paint job. Bob started out by painting everything with a base coat of white pearl. The red top coat is actually a number of coats of Kandy Cherry from the House of Kolor. Kenny Youngblood did the pinstripes and the eagle graphic on the sides of the tank. Like everything else about the bike, the paint job is very, very nice, yet still subdued.

Though the customizing that was done on this Springer may go unnoticed by some who see it, the bike's owner, Jerry Moreland, understands and appreciates all the changes. The subtle changes make this bike a very sophisticated Softail.

Next page
The dash face was cut from a chunk of aluminum and mounted to a support that is part of the Fat Bob tank. The ignition switch has been moved to the coil cover.

Previous page
The front fork is stock, just kicked out a little. Note the relocated headlight—a small change that makes a big difference in the look of the bike.

Here are more neat little tricks, like the flush-mount taillight. Red paint is a candy cherry sprayed over a white pearl base by Bob Bauder.

Chapter 6

Don Hotop

Don's House of Massage: The art of subtle changes

Don Hotop likes his bikes just right. First, they must run and run well. Second, everything on the bike needs to fit and contribute to the overall performance of the motorcycle. Don will do a lot of work just to achieve what other people might see as a small gain. Rather than using wild flames and radical new sheet metal, Don is more inclined to take an essentially good design, massage it to his own high standards, then put it all back together.

The orange FXR is a case in point. Though it looks great, especially in the late afternoon sun, the bike appears nearly stock. Don is sometimes disappointed with people who walk past the bike assuming it's just another FXR with a nice paint job.

Don started modifying this rubber-mount FXR design right at the beginning. What appears to be a stock Harley frame was cut up into eight separate pieces. At the front, the rake was changed from twenty-nine to thirty-three degrees. The rear of the frame came in for more subtle modifications. The stock Harley frame has a short stub that extends out past the triangular section at the rear of the frame. A combination frame cover and fender strut helps support the fender and hide the frame stub.

Rather than use a conventional fender strut, Don extended the frame back from the triangular section and used that extension to support the fender. The fender holes are tapped from the inside so that no bolt heads or nuts are visible from the outside. The total effect is a much cleaner and more sanitary look for the back of the bike. When he was doing these modifications to the rear of the frame, Don moved the upper shock mount forward both for better support and to lower the bike slightly.

After the frame was reassembled, Don started in on the body work and chassis. The gas tank seemed too wide, so it was cut in half the long way. Don sectioned the tank 2in in back and about 1in at the front. The rear fender is stock though the taillight is a one-off with the license plate hung neatly below it.

The chassis and hardware look normal and every-day, too, until you take the time to look closely. The Performance Machine calipers have been reworked on the mill, leaving them with milled slots across their polished surface. The slotted mounting brackets for the calipers came from Don's Massage Parlor, as did the matching derby cover, points cover, transmission cover, and air cleaner.

The brake lines are rather unusual, too. They look like plastic tubing. How could plastic be strong

Next page
The small De Soda diner with the neon signs is in Spearfish, South Dakota. The setting sun and the Dave Perewitz-applied candy tangerine paint job combine to give this FXR a warm glow.

The front rim is from Harley-Davidson. Like the rear, it is partly polished and partly painted in body color. Dual calipers from Performance Machine are polished, then milled to match the other accessories on the bike. Note the unique brake lines.

enough for the high pressure that hydraulic brakes are subjected to? The black plastic brake lines are actually the same material used inside a braided steel line. The fittings for these lines are special concoctions available only from Don's House of Massage.

The wheels are from Harley-Davidson, although they don't look like this on a stock FXR. Both the front and rear rims are polished to a high shine, while the rear center section and the front spokes are painted to match the body.

Set in the middle of Don's special frame is a mostly stock Evolution engine that was treated to the same kind of fine massaging as the rest of the bike. Mild rather than wild, Don installed a Sifton camshaft and pushrods and then did a little porting work on the

Next page
Success was achieved here, not by a single modification, but through an extensive collection of small changes—all of which work together to create a design that rings true.

The changes to Don's FXR are so well done they are hard to see. Note the missing fender struts, narrowed gas tank, hand-made taillight, and the milled covers.

The Evolution engine in Don's FXR is a mild street fighter. The camshaft is from Sifton. The heads have been ported, and the carburetor is a Model B from S&S. Getting the gas out of the cylinders is accomplished with a set of Supertrapp two-into-one pipes.

heads. While the engine was apart, the cases and cylinders were painted flat black. Then the fins and covers were either polished or chrome plated. The carburetor is a butterfly design, a Series B from S&S, while the exhaust pipes are a set of two-into-one pipes from Supertrapp.

Don wanted a paint job that was just right for the bike, so he called on the expertise of Dave Perewitz.

Profile: Don Hotop

Don Hotop is a big, hard-working Harley builder from Fort Madison, Iowa. Fort Madison is as far south as you can go and still be in Iowa. Listening to the drawl in Don's speech as he tells a story about some old Sportster, one thinks more of Missouri than Iowa. Good friends tease Don about his Iowa heritage. They harass poor Don and call his bikes "corn-fed" Harleys.

Like many bike builders, Don started out tinkering with go-carts and old beater cars at a very young age. As the years went by Don got more and more involved with cars. His first bikes were Triumphs, mostly stock 650 twins that he rode when he wasn't in one of his cars. In fact, it was just luck that he got involved in Harleys at all. That's because he won his first Harley in a game of "eight bawl."

As Don remembers it, "It was just the craziest thing. I played around in the pool hall a lot, and one day I had a bet going with this guy. He had an old side-hack Harley Forty-Five. The bet was fifty dollars. I won the game, and all he had was the Harley. I didn't think he'd even deliver the bike—but he did.

"So I got into Harleys right after that. The Forty-Five was a rat, aww-man, it was a terrible rat. You should have seen it. It was all bailing wire. That's what got me started. That old bike got about half-way around the block before the tranny blew out. So that was it—I had to fix it. Pretty soon I was fooling around with Harleys all the time instead of cars. I've been at it ever since."

Don learned how to build Harleys as he went along. Though he spent time in trade school studying tool and die work, that career never worked out. Don always found work in the factories and did his Harley building at night in his home shop.

His last factory job was doing maintenance work at the Chevron plant. He was "doing a lot of motorcycle work at night. My garage was full of Harleys all the time. I was making a few bucks on the side. When Chevron called and said I should come back to work, I said no. It was a big move, a chancy thing to do at the time."

Instead of going back to work at Chevron, Don scraped up every nickel he had and opened a very small Harley store. That was almost fifteen years ago, and he has no regrets. Though his current store is larger than the first, it's not what you'd call palatial. And though a lot of bikes and a lot of work come out of that store, Don runs it by himself most of the time. When asked how he gets all the work done, Don explains that he works "a lot of hours each week."

By his own admission, he is a nut for detail. Good workmanship is the thing that he respects and the kind of work that comes out of his shop. Yogi said that the game isn't over 'til it's over. Don would say that a motorcycle isn't finished until every little detail, every little bracket, is just right.

Over beers in a saloon near Sturgis, South Dakota, Don will go on at length, describing how the fabrication of a small clamp took a whole afternoon. Using his big hands to describe the shape, he explains, "I can't just rush through the little things. If it takes all day to do a little clamp or bracket, then I'll take all day. I hate to get rushed."

The man who hates to get rushed is currently working on a Softail. It's a Softail lowered and modified to meet Don's high standards. He has his own unique ideas for the rear suspension. He wants it low, just like everybody else, but he doesn't want it to drag on every corner and driveway.

It seems a long time ago now, since that one game of eight bawl. Was it luck or was it fate that got Don into the world of Harley-Davidsons? There is no absolute answer, but with all his enthusiasm for hand-built Harleys, it's hard to imagine Don Hotop doing anything else.

Don set out to capture the look and feel of bikes he built twenty years ago. Starting with a hardtail frame, springer fork, and Panhead engine, Don added a nice paint job by Shane Stevens.

The entire bike was boxed up and shipped to Massachusetts so Dave could perform his magic. The glowing effect was created in a two-step process using a white pearl as the base coat followed by the top coat of candy tangerine. The orange bars and pinstriping were applied last, followed by a final clear coat.

When the parts came back from the East Coast, Don assembled it all into a running motorcycle. Each part was carefully bolted in place. The wiring was carefully routed inside the frame. No detail was left undone.

Here sits a bike where everything fits and everything works. This bike sits as a sleeper, fooling people who walk by too fast. There's a lesson here for all of us. It's a lesson about good design, how sometimes less is

The rear view shows a bobbed fender, tombstone taillight, fat 140/90x16in Avon tire, small sissy bar, and fishtail pipes—another variation on an old theme.

more—and about the dangers of walking along so fast that we miss really nice work like that on Don's FXR.

Good Old Days

Remembering when

Don Hotop has been building Harleys for more than twenty years. He remembers well the good old days when everyone rode—or wanted to ride—a chopper. The formula was fairly simple: start with an old rigid frame, add a Panhead engine with a four-speed transmission, bolt a set of high bars known as ape-hangers onto the springer fork, and ride off into the sunset.

Don has come a long way since those days. Though he still builds bikes, most of them now are modern Harleys, neat designs built to go down the road. These Harleys are clean bikes with great paint, assembled with lavish attention to detail. Those old chopper bikes seemed like ancient history, until Don started to reminisce and wonder what it would be like to ride one of those old bikes again.

In late 1990 Don started serious reminiscing. He calls it "remembering when." Remembering when the bike he rode was a chopper. When most of his friends rode chopper-style Harleys. Looking back it seemed those choppers were great bikes. But memory has a way of sugar-coating the past. Looking back, the good old days often look better than they really were. Yet, the more he thought about it, the better those bikes looked. There was only one way to answer the question—only one way to find out if those old bikes were really as great as Don remembered.

As Don recalled, in the good old days you could build a nice chopper right off the shelf. The parts were all readily available. He wondered if he could still build one the same way.

The first part to arrive was the Santee hardtail frame. A conservative frame with only thirty-three degrees of fork rake and a 2in stretch. Next came the springer fork from Paughco, a completely polished one without any extra length. There was only one thing missing, and by doing a little horse trading, Don was able to find a stock 1964 Panhead engine.

He cleared an area in his Fort Madison, Iowa, shop, and between work on customers' bikes he assembled the new/old chopper. The frame, fork, and engine formed the basis for the new bike. Don sent the frame and the 3½gal Fat Bob tanks over to Shane Stevens for molding and paint.

Shane first knocked the lumps and bumps off the frame and then added just enough putty to completely smother all the seams. After the primer, Shane sprayed a gold base followed by candy apple red paint. The flames are subtle, done in candy orange and buried under multiple clear coats.

While Shane worked at smoothing the lumps on the frame and applying the multi-colored paint job, Don worked at rebuilding the Panhead engine. Don

enjoys a reputation for building bikes that are mechanically sound, and he was taking no chances with this old Panhead. Anything that looked suspect was replaced with brand new parts. Not content to put new pistons in bored out cylinders, Don bought new pistons *and* new cylinders. In fact, when Don finished up the engine and counted all the parts he'd bought, it turned out that the only original parts left in the engine were the bare heads and the bare cases!

Through the long Iowa winter, while the snow piled up outside the door, Don worked on the bike whenever he could. For wheels Don chose traditional spoked rims, a 21in in front and a 16in at the rear. Although the original choppers ran drum brakes, Don thought he could take this nostalgia thing only so far.

He bolted on disc brakes at both the front and the rear. The rotors are stainless steel units off the shelf at the store, squeezed by GMA calipers. Though this was supposed to be a bolt-together bike, the correct caliper mounting kits didn't exist, forcing Don to make his own. Before bolting them onto the bike, both the calipers and the brackets went to the plating shop for a quick dip in the chrome tank.

When it came to the rear fender, Don bought a fiberglass fender from the Arlen Ness catalog and modified it slightly to clear the chain. The small sissy bar that wraps up and around the fender was bent up from bar stock, then sent out to the plating shop along with some brackets and small parts.

As the snowbanks disappeared outside Don's shop, the red bike started to come together. It sat on a lift in the shop, and the regulars would check the progress from week to week. Most of them thought maybe Don had gone off the deep end. Why would he build this "old" bike when there were all these new zoomy bikes to design and build? Seig, the talented machinist who fabricates many of the parts for Don's scooters, was especially critical.

Don persevered, getting more and more excited about the project in spite of the criticism. With the Fat Bob tanks in place, the Avon tires mounted both front and rear, and the fishtail pipes mounted to the right side of the bike, Don could sit on the bike and almost feel the wind in his face. There were just a few details remaining, things like the tombstone taillight and the mandatory ape-hanger handle bars.

When the last snowbank finally disappeared on the north side of the building, it was time for the first road test. Don remembers that the ride was great. The bike worked well, felt even better, and got a lot of looks from people on the street and in cars. He expected a lot of flak from the guys at the shop but something else happened.

Next page
Sunset gives the multilayered paint a nice glow. The Fat Bob tanks hold 3½gal of gasoline. Choppers were pretty basic bikes, there isn't much here except what's essential to the machine's operation.

147

Previous page
This is it—a classic Panhead engine for a classic bike. No electric start, only a bicycle pedal and a strong right leg will do the trick. The engine has been completely rebuilt to stock 1964 specifications. A traditional air cleaner is a reproduction of the original and hides a Keihin, butterfly carburetor.

Once the bike ran, some of the guys asked if they could take it for a little putt. The effect on each rider was the same—they rolled back into the parking lot with a big grin from ear to ear. Earlier comments questioning Don's sanity for building such an old-fashioned bike were forgotten and never repeated. Suddenly everyone thought the new chopper was "neat, really a neat motorcycle."

Even Seig—loudest critic of all, rider of high-tech motorcycles from Germany, a man who never rode choppers in the old days—even Seig fell silent. In fact, during the festivities in Sturgis, Seig was often seen riding the new chopper. With a blue bandana wrapped around his head and that same damned grin, Seig rode the old Harley—and left his new BMW at the motel.

The polished springer fork is from Paughco. Note the nicely molded frame joints.

The bike was a major hit at Sturgis. It seemed that everybody could remember when. Gary Bang remembered better than anyone else how good those good old days were. In fact he took the bike home with him so he'd never forget.

He Rides a What?

Brotherly love

The Sportster seen here was built a few years ago, yet the lines and the bike still look very contemporary. With the possible exception of the shock and struts, there isn't much here that looks out of place today.

Don Hotop built the Sportster for his brother. He explained, "Fort Madison, Iowa, isn't a very big town. Here I was building and customizing Harleys in my shop, and my damned brother was riding all over town

This Sportster carries much of the detail and machine work for which Don is known.

on this new Suzuki. People wondered what was wrong with the bikes I built that my own brother wouldn't ride one. Finally I couldn't take it anymore. It seemed like the only way to get him off that Suzuki was to build him something better. I had this Sportster at the shop and I decided to build a nice bike for my brother out of that. The vision I had was a long, racy Sportster."

Don's first problem was building a Sportster to fit a large man well over six feet tall. More frame seemed

the logical answer, so Don welded on a new front frame section that stretched the frame a full 6in and gave it a rake of thirty-three degrees. The rest of the

Next page
The rear suspension is based on a pair of springs with minimal give. Note the bridged and plated swingarm, milled and plated sprocket cover, the neat fender struts, and the little air dam under the swingarm pivot.

Redwing fork carries mounting lugs for dual disc brake calipers and has been modified on Don's mill to match the rest of the bike.

frame was relieved of any bumps and brackets before the welds were molded smooth.

At the front of the frame, Don mounted a Redwing racing fork and trimmed it 2in. At the rear, the swingarm was reinforced with a bridge and then sent out for chrome plating. Don believes "you have to provide a lot of detail in the bike, so when someone stops to look they've got plenty to see. I figure that one certain thing, maybe the way you modified the gas tank, will get them to stop. And once they stop, all the little extra things you've done will keep them there looking and wondering, 'how did he do that?'"

The lower fork legs were polished, then taken over to the mill where three slots were milled into the metal itself. Similar milled patterns can be found in the dual Performance Machine front brake calipers. The rear caliper is from Performance Machine as well, and shows the same milled pattern seen in front.

The wheels used on both front and rear are spoked, a 16in at the rear with Dunlop rubber and a 19in at the front with an Avon tire.

A long bike needs a long gas tank—not the kind of thing you can order from the catalog. Don started with a Mustang tank and then s-t-r-e-t-c-h-e-d it with strips of sheet metal until it fit between the handlebars and the seat.

The bobbed rear fender came from Arlen Ness. The fender struts are another of Don's creations. Unable to find the correct seat on the shelf, Don had one made to fit the Sportster.

While the frame and body pieces were out being painted, Don pulled the engine completely apart for an update and rebuild. The bottom end was in good shape, so Don installed new bearings and left it at that. The connecting rods were replaced with a new set from S&S while the pistons were replaced with a pair of high-compression slugs from Arias. A firm believer in the old adage that if you want something done right, "you've got to do it yourself," Don did a valve job, then ported each exhaust and intake passage. To give the stock Harley valves a little extra lift, four Andrews camshafts were installed. A Bendix carburetor supplies fuel to the engine.

Not content to rebuild only the inside of the engine, Don reworked the outside as well. Covers on both sides were chrome plated, as were the cylinder fins and rocker boxes. Everywhere you look there are slots, either milled into or through the covers themselves. The generator housing seemed an ugly piece no matter what Don might do to it, so he made his own, from aluminum, with milled slots on either end to match the rest of the detail work.

Don chose Shane Stevens to finish the metal work on the bike and apply the final paint. After each weld was ground smooth and filled, Shane applied multiple coats of wild cherry from the House of Kolor. The final touch was the blue highlights and a clear coat.

Everyone who hears the story of the Sportster built to replace the Suzuki wants to know: Did it work? Yes, Don's brother was convinced to give up that nasty old rice-grinder and take off on a real American motorcycle. Later though, the Sporty seemed to slip through his hands and today it belongs to Shane Stevens, the man who painted it. That may not be all bad since Shane truly appreciates the bike—and there's no chance in hell that he's going to trade it for a Suzuki.

Index